SELECTIONS FROM
Better Homes and Gardens

NEW COOK BOOK

A BANTAM PREMIUM BOOK

BANTAM BOOKS
TORONTO · NEW YORK · LONDON · SYDNEY

*This Bantam Premium Book
features selected text from
Better Homes and Gardens® New Cook Book,
revised edition, published by
Meredith Corporation, Des Moines, IA, 1981.*

SELECTIONS FROM BETTER HOMES AND GARDENS® NEW COOK BOOK
*A Bantam Book / published by arrangement with
Meredith Corporation*

*All rights reserved.
Copyright © 1930, 1963, 1981, 1992
by Meredith Corporation, Des Moines, Iowa.
This book may not be reproduced in whole or in part, by
mimeograph or any other means, without permission.
For information address: Meredith Corporation,
1716 Locust Street, Des Moines, IA 30336*

Bantam Books are published by Bantam Books, Inc.
Its trademark, consisting of the words "Bantam
Books" and the portrayal of a rooster, is Registered
in U.S. Patent and Trademark Office and in other
countries, Marca Registrada. Bantam Books, Inc.,
666 Fifth Avenue, New York, New York 10103.

PRINTED IN THE UNITED STATES OF AMERICA

CONTENTS

Appetizers & Snacks	5
Barbecue	13
Beverages	23
Breads	27
Cakes	39
Candy	49
Cookies	53
Desserts	63
Eggs & Cheese	71
Fish & Seafood	81
Meat	91
Pies	109
Poultry	119
Rice, Pasta & Cereal	133
Salads & Dressings	141
Sauces & Relishes	155
Soups & Stews	163
Vegetables	173
Index	185

APPETIZERS & SNACKS

Prepare some of your snacks or appetizers ahead of time to avoid a last-minute rush. After preparation, wrap or cover foods so they are airtight (use moisture-vaporproof material for the freezer). Chill or freeze the food quickly. Use refrigerated foods within 24 hours or within the time given in the recipe to avoid loss of flavor and quality.

SHRIMP-CUCUMBER APPETIZER SPREAD

- 1 3-ounce package cream cheese, softened
- 2 tablespoons mayonnaise or salad dressing
- 1 tablespoon catsup
- 1 teaspoon prepared mustard
  Dash garlic powder
- 1 4½-ounce can shrimp, drained and chopped
- ¼ cup finely chopped cucumber
- 1 teaspoon finely chopped onion
  Melba toast

In a mixing bowl stir together the cream cheese and mayonnaise or salad dressing; stir in catsup, mustard, and garlic powder. Stir in chopped shrimp, cucumber, and onion. Spread mixture over melba toast. Garnish with additional shrimp and cucumber, if desired. Makes 1¼ cups spread.

Appetizer Juices

For a light and nonfilling appetizer, serve a small glass of juice. Try an icy-cold fruit juice garnished with fresh fruit or a mint sprig. Or, heat fruit juice (or a mixture of fruit juices) with cloves and stick cinnamon for a warming appetizer.

Vegetable juices such as tomato, carrot, or vegetable juice cocktail served cold or hot also are excellent meal starters. If desired, add herbs, seasoned salt, Worcestershire sauce, or bottled hot pepper sauce for extra spiciness.

BAKED HAM-STUFFED MUSHROOMS

- 24 fresh mushrooms, 1½ to 2 inches in diameter
- ¼ cup chopped green onion
- 1 tablespoon butter or margarine
- 2 teaspoons all-purpose flour
- ¼ teaspoon dried savory, crushed
- 2 tablespoons dry white wine
- ½ cup finely chopped, fully cooked ham
- 2 tablespoons grated Parmesan cheese
- ¼ cup fine dry bread crumbs   Oven 350°

Wash mushrooms; drain. Remove stems from mushrooms; reserve caps. Chop stems to make 1 cup. Cook chopped stems and green onion in butter or margarine just till tender. Stir in flour, savory, and ⅛ teaspoon *pepper*; add wine and 2 tablespoons *water*. Cook and stir till thickened and bubbly; stir in ham and Parmesan. Fill mushroom caps with ham mixture. Place mushrooms in a 15 × 10 × 1-inch baking pan. Top with bread crumbs. Bake in a 350° oven for 15 to 20 minutes or till tender. Makes 24.

EGG SALAD TRIANGLES

  4 hard-cooked eggs, chopped
  2 tablespoons chopped pimiento-stuffed olives
  1 tablespoon finely chopped green onion
  3 tablespoons mayonnaise or salad dressing
  2 teaspoons prepared mustard
  5 slices white sandwich bread
    Sliced pimiento-stuffed olives (optional)

Combine chopped eggs, chopped olives, and green onion; stir in mayonnaise or salad dressing and mustard. Remove crusts from bread, if desired. Spread each slice of bread with about ¼ *cup* of the egg mixture. Cut each slice of bread diagonally into quarters. If desired, garnish each sandwich with sliced pimiento-stuffed olives. Makes 20 sandwiches.

PARTY HAM SANDWICHES

  1 4½-ounce can deviled ham
  ¼ cup finely chopped celery
  ¼ cup finely chopped dill pickle
  1 tablespoon mayonnaise or salad dressing
  4 slices firm-textured white bread
  4 slices firm-textured rye bread
  1 4-ounce container whipped cream cheese
    Snipped parsley
    Pimiento strips

Combine deviled ham, celery, dill pickle, and mayonnaise or salad dressing. Cover; chill. Remove crusts from bread, if desired. Spread white bread slices with ham mixture, top with rye bread slices. Frost tops with cream cheese. Cut each sandwich diagonally into quarters. Decorate sandwiches with parsley or pimiento. Makes 16 sandwiches.

CHEESE-WINE LOG

   2 cups shredded sharp cheddar cheese, softened
   1 3-ounce package cream cheese, softened
   ⅓ cup dry white wine
   1 tablespoon finely chopped green onion
   1 teaspoon prepared horseradish
   1 2½-ounce package (about 1 cup) smoked beef, finely snipped
   Assorted crackers

In a small mixer bowl beat softened cheeses till nearly smooth; gradually beat in wine. Add onion and prepared horseradish. Chill mixture about 1 hour or till slightly firm. Shape mixture into 2 logs, each about 6 inches long. Roll each in *half* of the beef. Wrap and chill till ready to serve. Serve with crackers. Makes 2.

CHEESE BALL

   1 8-ounce package cream cheese, softened
   ½ cup dairy sour cream
   ¼ cup butter or margarine, softened
   2 tablespoons finely chopped pimiento
   1 tablespoon snipped parsley
   1 teaspoon grated onion
   ⅓ cup finely chopped nuts
   ⅓ cup snipped parsley

Combine cream cheese, sour cream, and butter or margarine; beat with electric mixer till fluffy. Stir in pimiento, 1 tablespoon parsley, and onion. Chill. Shape into a ball. Coat with nuts and ⅓ cup parsley. Makes about 1¾ cups.

Swiss Cheese-Ham Spread: Prepare as above, *except* omit nuts and ⅓ cup parsley. Have 1 cup shredded

Swiss cheese at room temperature. Combine Swiss cheese, cheese ball mixture, one 3-ounce can *deviled ham*, and 1 teaspoon *prepared mustard*. Beat till almost smooth. Cover; chill. Makes 3 cups.

COCKTAIL MEATBALLS

- 1 beaten egg
- 2 tablespoons fine dry bread crumbs
- 2 tablespoons thinly sliced green onion
- 2 tablespoons finely chopped green pepper
- ¼ teaspoon dried thyme, crushed
- ½ pound lean ground beef
- Cooking oil
- Tangy Cranberry Sauce

Combine egg, bread crumbs, green onion, green pepper, thyme, ½ teaspoon *salt*, and dash *pepper*. Add ground beef; mix well. Shape beef mixture into ¾-inch meatballs. (Allow meatballs to stand at room temperature 30 minutes before cooking.)

Pour cooking oil into a metal fondue cooker to no more than ½ capacity or to a depth of 2 inches. Heat over range to 350°. Add 1 teaspoon *salt* to the hot oil. Transfer cooker to a fondue burner. Spear individual meatballs with a fondue fork; cook in hot oil about 1 minute or till browned. Transfer meatballs to a dinner fork; dip into warm Tangy Cranberry Sauce. Makes about 40 meatballs.

Tangy Cranberry Sauce: Combine one 8-ounce can *jellied cranberry sauce*, 3 tablespoons *bottled steak sauce*, 2 teaspoons *brown sugar*, 2 teaspoons *cooking oil*, and 1 teaspoon *prepared mustard*. Beat till smooth with a rotary beater. Heat through. Makes 2 cups.

OYSTERS ROCKEFELLER

  1 10-ounce package frozen chopped spinach
 24 oysters in shells
  2 tablespoons chopped onion
  2 tablespoons snipped parsley
  2 tablespoons butter or margarine, melted
 ½ teaspoon salt
    Several drops bottled hot pepper sauce
 ¼ cup fine dry breadcrumbs
  1 tablespoon butter or margarine, melted
    Rock salt   Oven 450°

Cook spinach according to package directions. Drain well; press out excess water. Set aside. Thoroughly wash oysters in shells. Open each with an oyster knife or other blunt-tipped knife. With a knife remove oysters and dry. Discard flat top shells; thoroughly wash deep bottom shells. Place each oyster in a shell half.

Stir together cooked spinach, chopped onion, snipped parsley, 2 tablespoons melted butter or margarine, salt, hot pepper sauce, and dash *pepper*. Top *each* oyster shell with *1 tablespoon* of the spinach mixture.

In a small bowl toss together bread crumbs and the 1 tablespoon melted butter or margarine. Sprinkle about ½ *teaspoon* of the buttered crumbs over *each* spinach-topped oyster.

Line a shallow baking pan with rock salt to about ½-inch depth. (*Or*, use crumpled aluminum foil to keep shells from tipping.) Arrange oysters atop salt or crumpled foil. Bake in a 450° oven about 10 minutes or till heated through. Makes 4 servings.

CRUNCH PARTY MIX

- 1 cup cooking oil
- 2 tablespoons Worcestershire sauce
- 1 teaspoon garlic salt
- 1 teaspoon seasoned salt
- Several drops bottled hot pepper sauce
- 7 cups round toasted oat cereal (6 ounces)
- 5 cups small pretzels (8 ounces)
- 3 cups salted mixed nuts (1 pound)
- 3 cups bite-sized shredded wheat squares (6 ounces)
- ¼ cup grated Parmesan cheese   Oven 250°

In a saucepan heat together the oil, Worcestershire, garlic salt, seasoned salt, and hot pepper sauce. In a large roasting pan combine the oat cereal, pretzels, nuts, and shredded wheat squares. Stir oil mixture well; drizzle over cereal mixture, tossing to coat evenly. Bake in a 250° oven for 2 hours, stirring every 30 minutes. Remove from oven; sprinkle with Parmesan; toss lightly. Makes about 16 cups.

CREAMY DILL DIP

- 1 cup dairy sour cream
- 1 cup mayonnaise or salad dressing
- 1 tablespoon minced dried onion
- 1 tablespoon dried dillweed
- ½ teaspoon seasoned salt
- Assorted fresh vegetable dippers or crisp crackers

Thoroughly combine sour cream, mayonnaise or salad dressing, minced dried onion, dillweed, and seasoned salt. Cover and chill thoroughly to blend flavors. Serve with fresh vegetable dippers or crackers. Makes 2 cups.

FLUFFY FRUIT DIP

> 1 cup dairy sour cream
> ⅓ cup apricot or peach preserves, or orange marmalade
> ¼ cup finely chopped walnuts
> 2 to 3 tablespoons milk
> Assorted fresh or canned fruit dippers, chilled

In a small bowl combine sour cream, preserves or marmalade (cut up any large pieces of fruit), and walnuts; mix well. Stir in enough milk to make mixture of dipping consistency; chill. To serve, insert wooden picks into chilled fruit pieces. Dunk fruit into chilled dip. Makes 1½ cups dip.

CREAMY ONION DIP

> 1 cup dairy sour cream
> ½ cup mayonnaise or salad dressing
> 2 tablespoons regular onion soup mix
> 2 tablespoons snipped parsley
> Potato chips, corn chips, or crisp crackers

Thoroughly combine sour cream, mayonnaise or salad dressing, onion soup mix, and parsley. Cover; chill till serving time. Serve with your choice of chips or crackers. Makes 1½ cups.

Blue Cheese-Onion Dip: Prepare Creamy Onion Dip as above, *except* stir in ½ cup crumbled *blue cheese*, ⅓ cup chopped *walnuts*, and 2 tablespoons *milk*. Makes 2 cups.

BARBECUE

Becoming familiar with basic barbecuing techniques makes cooking *outdoors* over the charcoal grill even more pleasant.

Determine the approximate amount of briquettes you'll need. Small, short-cooking foods need fewer briquettes than thicker meat cuts. Mound briquettes and start them with liquid lighter or jelly fire starter, following label directions. Or, omit the fuel fire starters and use an electric starter. *Don't use gasoline or kerosene!* Once started, let the coals burn until they die down to a glow.

Arrange the coals with long-handled tongs. For foods cooked flat, such as steaks, chops, and burgers, spread coals over the entire firebox. Place coals about ½ inch apart. For kebabs, line up coals in parallel rows, placing some around edges of grill. Place kebabs on grate over spaces between briquette rows.

To check the temperature of the coals, hold your hand, palm side down, above the coals at the distance the food will be cooking. Start counting "one thousand one, one thousand two," etc. If you need to remove your hand after 2 seconds, the coals are *Hot*; 3 seconds, *Medium-hot*; 4 seconds, *Medium*; and 5 or 6 seconds, *Slow*.

The cooking times for chicken, ribs, and chops can be shortened with the use of a microwave oven. Just partially micro-cook these foods before placing them on the grill.

QUICK GARLIC CUBED STEAKS

- ¼ cup butter or margarine
- 2 tablespoons Worcestershire sauce
- 2 tablespoons lemon juice
- 1 teaspoon finely snipped parsley
- ½ teaspoon celery salt
- 1 clove garlic, minced
- 6 beef cubed steaks
- 6 slices French bread, toasted

In a saucepan melt butter; stir in Worcestershire, lemon juice, parsley, celery salt, and garlic. Brush butter mixture on both sides of steaks. Place steaks in a wire grill basket. Grill over *hot* coals for 1 to 2 minutes. Turn basket over and grill for 1 to 2 minutes more. Season steaks with salt and pepper. Place each steak atop a toasted bread slice. Spoon remaining butter mixture over steaks. Serves 6.

BEEF TERIYAKI

- 1½ pounds boneless beef tenderloin or sirloin steak
- ½ cup soy sauce
- 2 tablespoons cooking oil
- 2 tablespoons molasses
- 2 teaspoons dry mustard
- 1 teaspoon ground ginger
- 4 cloves garlic, halved

Partially freeze beef; thinly slice across grain into approximately 3-inch strips. For marinade, combine soy sauce, oil, molasses, mustard, ginger, garlic, and ¼ cup *water*; mix well. Add meat to marinade; let stand 15 minutes at room temperature. Drain meat, reserving marinade. Thread meat strips accordion style on 12 skewers. If desired, halve preserved kumquats crosswise and add a kumquat half to the end of each skewer. Grill skewers over *hot* coals 5 to 7 minutes or to desired doneness. Turn and baste occasionally with marinade. Serves 6.

ONION-STUFFED STEAK

- 2 beef porterhouse steaks, cut 1½ inches thick (about 1½ pounds each), or 1 beef sirloin steak, cut 1½ inches thick (about 2 to 2½ pounds)
- ½ cup sliced green onion
- 1 large clove garlic, minced
- 3 tablespoons butter or margarine
  Dash celery salt
- ¼ cup dry red wine
- 2 tablespoons soy sauce
- 1 cup sliced fresh mushrooms

Slash fat edges of steak at 1-inch intervals (don't cut into meat). Slice pockets in each side of meat, cutting almost to bone. In a skillet cook onion and garlic in *1 tablespoon* of the butter. Add celery salt and dash *pepper*. Stuff pockets with onion mixture; skewer closed. Mix wine and soy sauce; brush on meat. Grill over *medium-hot* coals for 8 to 10 minutes; brush often with soy mixture. Turn; grill 8 to 10 minutes more for rare. Brush often with soy mixture. In a small skillet cook mushrooms in the remaining 2 tablespoons butter till tender. Slice steak across grain. Pass mushrooms to spoon atop steak. Serves 6.

16 Barbecue

PINEAPPLE-GLAZED CHICKEN

- 1 8¼-ounce can crushed pineapple
- ½ cup chili sauce or hot-style catsup
- 2 tablespoons brown sugar
- 1 tablespoon prepared mustard
- 2 2½- to 3-pound broiler-fryer chickens, halved lengthwise
- Cooking oil
- Salt

For sauce, drain pineapple, reserving ¼ cup syrup. Combine pineapple, reserved syrup, chili sauce or catsup, sugar, and mustard.

Break wing, hip, and drumstick joints of chickens; twist wing tips under back. Brush chickens lightly with oil; season with salt. Grill chickens over *medium-hot* coals, bone side down, for 25 to 30 minutes or till bone side is well browned. Turn chickens. Grill 20 minutes more. Turn chickens again. Spoon sauce atop. Grill 5 to 10 minutes more or till chickens are done. Makes 12 servings.

GLAZED HAM SLICE

- ½ cup hot-style catsup
- ½ cup apricot preserves, pineapple preserves, or orange marmalade
- 2 tablespoons finely chopped onion
- 1 tablespoon cooking oil
- 1 tablespoon prepared mustard
- 1 teaspoon Worcestershire sauce
- 1 1½- to 2-pound fully cooked ham slice, cut 1 inch thick

For glaze, in a saucepan combine catsup, preserves or marmalade, onion, oil, mustard, and Worcestershire sauce. Simmer, uncovered, for 5 minutes, stirring once or twice.

Slash fat edge of ham slice to prevent curling. Grill ham slice over *medium* coals for 10 to 15 minutes; brush lightly with glaze. Turn ham and grill 10 to 15 minutes more or till done, brushing with glaze the last 10 minutes. Reheat glaze in a small saucepan on edge of grill. To serve, cut ham into slices; pass heated glaze. Makes 6 to 8 servings.

CORN-STUFFED PORK CHOPS

- 6 pork loin chops, cut 1½ inches thick
- ¼ cup chopped green pepper
- ¼ cup chopped onion
- 1 tablespoon butter or margarine
- 1 beaten egg
- 1½ cups toasted bread cubes
- ½ cup cooked whole kernel corn
- 2 tablespoons chopped pimiento
- ½ teaspoon salt
- ¼ teaspoon ground cumin
  Dash pepper

Cut a pocket in each chop by cutting from fat side almost to bone edge. Season cavity of each with a little salt and pepper.

For stuffing, in a small saucepan cook green pepper and onion in butter till tender but not brown. Combine egg, bread cubes, corn, pimiento, salt, cumin, and pepper. Pour cooked pepper and onion over bread cube mixture; toss lightly. Spoon about ¼ *cup* of the stuffing into each pork chop. Securely fasten pocket opening with wooden picks. Grill over *medium* coals about 20 minutes. Turn meat; grill 15 to 20 minutes more or till done. Before serving, remove picks. Serves 6.

APPLE-PEANUT-BUTTERED PORK STEAKS

½ cup apple butter
2 tablespoons peanut butter
¼ teaspoon finely shredded orange peel
2 tablespoons orange juice
4 pork shoulder blade steaks, cut ¾ inch thick (2 pounds)

Blend apple butter into peanut butter; add orange peel and juice. Season steaks with a little salt and pepper. Grill over *medium* coals about 15 minutes. Turn steaks; brush with apple butter mixture. Grill 15 to 20 minutes more. Brush on remaining mixture. Serves 4.

GRILLED SALMON STEAKS

3 fresh or frozen salmon steaks or other fish steaks (1 to 1½ inches thick)
½ cup cooking oil
¼ cup snipped parsley
¼ cup lemon juice
2 tablespoons grated onion
1 teaspoon dry mustard
¼ teaspoon salt

Thaw fish, if frozen. Place fish in a shallow dish. For marinade, combine oil, parsley, lemon juice, onion, mustard, salt, and dash *pepper*. Pour over fish. Marinate, covered, in the refrigerator 6 hours. Drain, reserving marinade. Place fish in a well-greased wire grill basket. Grill over *medium-hot* coals 8 to 10 minutes or till fish is lightly browned. Baste with marinade and turn. Brush again with marinade; grill 8 to 10 minutes more or till fish flakes easily when tested with a fork. Makes 6 servings.

FOIL-BARBECUED SHRIMP

- 2 pounds fresh or frozen large shrimp, shelled and deveined
- 6 tablespoons butter or margarine
- ½ cup snipped parsley
- ¾ teaspoon curry powder
- 1 clove garlic, minced
- ½ teaspoon salt
- Dash pepper

Thaw shrimp, if frozen. In a saucepan melt butter; stir in parsley, curry powder, garlic, salt, and pepper. Add shrimp; stir to coat. Divide shrimp mixture equally among six 12×18-inch pieces of heavy-duty foil. Fold foil around shrimp, sealing the edges well.

Grill foil-wrapped shrimp packages over *hot* coals about 8 minutes. Turn and grill 7 to 8 minutes more or till done. Serve in foil packages, if desired. Makes 6 servings.

POLISH SAUSAGE-KRAUTERS

- 8 Polish sausages or large frankfurters
- 1 8-ounce can sauerkraut, drained and snipped
- ¼ cup chili sauce
- 2 tablespoons finely chopped onion
- 1 teaspoon caraway seed

Slit sausages or frankfurters lengthwise, cutting almost to ends and only ¾ of the way through. Combine sauerkraut, chili sauce, onion, and caraway seed. Stuff about *2 tablespoons* of the mixture into the slit of each sausage or frankfurter; secure with wooden picks. Grill over *hot* coals for 10 to 12 minutes, turning frequently. Remove picks. Serve in frankfurter buns, if desired. Serves 4.

WINE-SAUCED SHOULDER CHOPS

- ¼ cup thinly sliced green onion
- 1 2-ounce can (¼ cup) sliced pimiento, drained and chopped
- ½ teaspoon dried oregano, crushed
- ¼ teaspoon dried tarragon, crushed
- ¼ teaspoon lemon pepper or pepper
- 2 tablespoons olive or cooking oil
- 1 tablespoon cornstarch
- 1 tablespoon Worcestershire sauce
- ½ cup dry white wine
- 8 lamb shoulder chops, cut ¾ to 1 inch thick

For sauce, cook onion, pimiento, herbs, and pepper in hot oil till onion is tender. Combine cornstarch, Worcestershire, and ⅓ cup *cold water*; stir into onion mixture. Cook and stir till bubbly. Add wine. Keep sauce warm.

Grill chops over *medium* coals for 10 to 12 minutes. Turn chops; grill 10 to 12 minutes more or until done, brushing frequently with sauce. Pass remaining sauce. Serves 8.

GRILLED ACORN SQUASH

- 3 medium acorn squash
- 2 tablespoons butter or margarine
- 2 tablespoons brown sugar
- 2 tablespoons water
- Brown sugar
- 1 apple, cut into wedges

Rinse squash. Cut in half lengthwise; remove seeds. Prick insides with the tines of a fork; season cavities with salt and pepper. Add *1 teaspoon* each of butter, brown sugar, and water to each squash. Wrap each half, cut side up, in a 12×18-inch piece of heavy-duty foil; seal securely. Place cut side up on grill. Grill over *medium* coals 50 to 60 minutes or till tender. Open foil. Stir to fluff squash; sprinkle with additional brown sugar. Top with wedges of apple. Makes 6 servings.

ITALIAN-SEASONED VEGETABLE KEBABS

- 12 fresh large mushrooms
- 2 small zucchini, cut into 1-inch bias-sliced pieces
- 3 tablespoons Italian salad dressing
- 2 tablespoons lemon juice
- 1 teaspoon Worcestershire sauce
- ¼ teaspoon salt
- 12 cherry tomatoes

Pour some boiling water over mushrooms in a bowl. Let stand 1 minute; drain. On four skewers alternately thread mushrooms and zucchini. Combine Italian salad dressing, lemon juice, Worcestershire sauce, and salt. Grill kebabs over *medium* coals about 12 minutes, turning and brushing often with salad dressing mixture. Thread cherry tomatoes on ends of skewers; grill 5 to 8 minutes more or till heated through, turning and brushing often with salad dressing mixture. Makes 4 servings.

GRILLED BREAD FIX-UPS

Match a bread or roll with a spread—
French or Italian Bread: Cut a *1-pound loaf* into 1-inch diagonal slices, cutting to, but not through, bottom crust. Spread your choice of spread between every other slice of bread. Wrap loosely in heavy-duty foil. Place on edge of grill. Grill over *slow* coals about

15 minutes or till heated through, turning frequently.*
Makes about 15 servings.

Dinner or Hard Rolls: Split 10 to 12 *dinner rolls* in half. (For hard rolls, split each roll horizontally, cutting to, but not through, opposite side of roll.) Spread your choice of spread on cut surfaces of each roll; reassemble rolls. Wrap loosely in heavy-duty foil. Grill over *slow* coals for about 10 minutes or till heated through, turning twice.* Makes 10 to 12 servings.

Rye or Wheat Bread: Spread your choice of spread on one side of 12 *bread slices*. Place slices together, forming 6 sandwiches; stack sandwiches. Wrap loosely in heavy-duty foil. Grill over *slow* coals for 12 minutes or till heated through.* Pull slices apart to serve. Makes 12 servings.

Garlic Spread: Stir together 6 tablespoons *butter*, softened, and ½ teaspoon *garlic powder*.

Parmesan Spread: Combine 6 tablespoons *butter*, softened; ¼ cup grated *Parmesan cheese*; and 1 tablespoon snipped *chives*.

Cheesy Butter Spread: Cream together ¾ cup shredded *Swiss, cheddar, Monterey Jack*, or *American cheese*; ¼ cup *butter or margarine*, softened; 2 tablespoons finely snipped *parsley*; and 2 teaspoons *prepared horseradish*.

Herbed Spread: Cream together 6 tablespoons *butter*, softened; ½ teaspoon dried *marjoram*, crushed; ½ teaspoon dried *thyme*, crushed; and ¼ teaspoon *garlic powder*.

*Note: Or, wrap loosely in foil and place on a baking sheet. Bake in a 350° oven for 15 to 20 minutes or till heated through.

BEVERAGES

There are as many ways to use and serve beverages as there are recipes for them. With some imagination, a beverage can be an intriguing accompaniment to a meal, an appetizer, a dessert, or simply a refreshment to enjoy by itself. Explore the many varieties offered to you in this chapter.

Several recipes that call for carbonated beverages as ingredients recommend that you slowly pour the carbonated beverage down the side of the punch bowl or glass. This will prevent any loss of carbonation when adding the beverage to the other ingredients.

STRAWBERRY SPRITZER

- 3 10-ounce packages frozen sliced strawberries
- 6 cups white grape juice
- 1 28-ounce bottle carbonated water, chilled

Let strawberries stand at room temperature 20 minutes. Place 2 of the *undrained* packages of strawberries in a blender container. Cover and blend till smooth. In a large punch bowl or pitcher combine blended strawberries, grape juice, and remaining *undrained* package of strawberries.

To serve, slowly pour in carbonated water; stir gently to mix. Add red food coloring, if desired. Makes 24 (4-ounce) servings.

APRICOT SWIZZLE

 2 cups water
 1 12-ounce can apricot nectar
 1 6-ounce can frozen lemonade concentrate, thawed
 ¼ cup sugar
 2 tablespoons instant tea powder
   Ice cubes
 1 28-ounce bottle ginger ale, chilled

Combine water, nectar, lemonade concentrate, sugar, and tea powder; stir till sugar and tea dissolve. Pour over ice in a punch bowl. Slowly pour in ginger ale; stir gently to mix. Makes about 7 (8-ounce) servings.

PARTY PUNCH BASE

 ⅓ cup sugar
 12 inches stick cinnamon, broken
 ½ teaspoon whole cloves
 3 cups apple juice, chilled
 1 12-ounce can apricot nectar, chilled
 ¼ cup lemon juice

In a small saucepan combine sugar, cinnamon, cloves, and ½ cup *water*; bring to boiling. Reduce heat; cover and simmer 10 minutes. Strain out spices and discard. Chill. Combine with apple juice, apricot nectar, and lemon juice. Makes 5 cups Party Punch Base. Use in the following party punches:

White Wine Punch: Prepare Party Punch Base as above. In a punch bowl combine Party Punch Base and two 750-milliliter bottles of chilled *dry white wine*. Stir to mix. Makes 23 (4-ounce) servings.

Nonalcoholic Punch: Prepare Party Punch Base as at left. Combine Party Punch Base with two 28-ounce bottles of chilled *lemon-lime or grapefruit carbonated beverage*. Makes 22 (4-ounce) servings.

FRUIT COOLER

- 1 envelope unsweetened raspberry-flavored soft drink mix
- ½ cup sugar
- 1 46-ounce can unsweetened pineapple juice
- ½ cup orange juice
- ¼ cup lemon juice
- Ice cubes

Add raspberry-flavored soft drink mix and sugar to pineapple juice. Stir to dissolve. Add remaining fruit juices. Chill. Serve over ice. Makes about 6 (8-ounce) servings.

FRUIT-FLAVORED FLOAT

- 1 cup sugar
- 1 envelope unsweetened lemon-lime- or cherry-flavored soft drink mix
- 2 cups milk
- 1 quart vanilla ice cream
- 1 28-ounce bottle carbonated water, chilled

Combine sugar and fruit-flavored soft drink mix. Add milk; stir to dissolve sugar. Pour mixture into 8 tall glasses. Spoon about ½ *cup* of the ice cream into each glass. Slowly pour in the chilled carbonated water to fill each glass. Stir gently to mix. (Or, mix and serve in a large punch bowl, if desired.) Makes about 8 (8-ounce) servings.

HOT MULLED CIDER

- 8 cups apple cider or apple juice
- ½ cup packed brown sugar
- Dash ground nutmeg
- 6 inches stick cinnamon
- 1 teaspoon whole allspice
- 1 teaspoon whole cloves
- 8 thin orange wedges or slices
- 8 whole cloves

In a large saucepan combine apple cider or juice, brown sugar, and nutmeg. *For spice bag*, place cinnamon, allspice, and the 1 teaspoon cloves in cheesecloth and tie; add to cider mixture. Bring to boiling. Reduce heat; cover and simmer 10 minutes. Remove spice bag and discard. Serve cider in mugs with a clove-studded orange wedge in each. Makes 8 (8-ounce) servings.

DESSERT COFFEE

- ½ cup hot strong coffee
- Desired coffee flavoring (see choices below)
- Whipped cream
- Ground cinnamon or nutmeg

In a coffee cup or mug stir together hot coffee and desired flavoring. Top with a dollop of whipped cream; sprinkle with cinnamon or nutmeg. Makes 1 (6-ounce) serving.

Café Israel: Stir 2 tablespoons *chocolate-flavored syrup* and 2 tablespoons *orange liqueur* into coffee.

Café Columbian: Stir 2 tablespoons *coffee liqueur* and 1 tablespoon *chocolate-flavored syrup* into coffee.

Café Almond: Stir 2 tablespoons *Amaretto* into coffee.

BREADS

Yeast Breads

When making yeast breads, you'll want your loaves to look and taste extra special. Below are some helpful hints we recommend for achieving a perfect product every time.

Although you can still make bread the conventional "soften-the-yeast" way, consider the newer easy-mix method. It eliminates the yeast-softening step since you combine the dry yeast directly with the flour.

When the recipe gives a range on the amount of flour, start by adding the smaller amount. And remember, flour used in kneading is also part of this measured amount.

Don't place dough in a hot area to rise because excessive heat will kill the yeast. A good spot is in an unheated oven with a large pan of hot water set on the lower rack under the bowl of dough. The optimum rising temperature is 80°.

Do not add flour after the rising starts. This produces dark streaks and a coarse texture.

Don't let loaves rise too long or to the top of the pan. If the dough rises much over twice its original size, the cell walls become thin; since the dough rises further in the oven, the cells may collapse and the bread may fall.

Before baking, gently brush the top of the loaf with shortening, butter, margarine, or oil for a browner crust. Brush with milk, water, or beaten egg for a crispy and shiny crust. For a softer crust, brush the top with butter or margarine after baking.

BATTER ROLLS

Oven 375°

In a large mixer bowl combine 2 cups *all-purpose flour* and 1 package *active dry yeast*. In a saucepan heat 1¼ cups *milk*, ½ cup *shortening*, ¼ cup *sugar*, and 1 teaspoon *salt* just till warm (115° to 120°) and shortening is almost melted; stir constantly. Add to flour mixture; add 1 *egg*. Beat at low speed of electric mixer for ½ minute, scraping sides of bowl constantly. Beat 3 minutes at high speed. Add 1¼ cups *all-purpose flour*; beat at low speed about 2 minutes or till batter is smooth.

Cover; let rise in a warm place till double (about 1 hour). Beat down with a wooden spoon. Let rest 5 minutes. Spoon into greased muffin cups, filling each half full. Cover; let rise till nearly double (about 30 minutes). Brush tops lightly with *milk*; sprinkle with 1 tablespoon *poppy seed or sesame seed*, if desired. Bake in a 375° oven 15 to 18 minutes. Makes 18.

PEASANT BREAD

Oven 375°

In a large mixer bowl combine 2 cups *all-purpose flour* and 2 packages *active dry yeast*. Heat 1¾ cups *water*, ¼ cup *dark molasses*, 2 tablespoons *cooking oil*, and 2 teaspoons *salt* just till warm (115° to 120°); stir constantly. Add to flour mixture. Beat at low speed of electric mixer ½ minute, scraping bowl. Beat 3 minutes at high speed. Stir in 1½ cups *rye flour*, ½ cup *whole bran cereal*, ⅓ cup *yellow cornmeal*, 1 tablespoon *caraway seed*, and as much of 1 to 1½ cups *all-purpose flour* as you can mix in with a spoon. On a lightly floured surface knead in enough remaining all-purpose flour to make a moderately stiff dough that is smooth and elastic (6 to 8 minutes total). Shape into a ball in a greased bowl; turn once. Cover; let rise in a warm place till double (1 to 1¼ hours).

Punch down; turn out onto a floured surface. Divide in half. Cover; let rest 10 minutes. Shape into 2 loaves; place in two greased 8×4×2-inch loaf pans. Cover; let rise till nearly double (30 to 45 minutes). Bake in a 375° oven 35 to 40 minutes. Makes 2 loaves.

CHEESE BREAD

Oven 350°

In a large mixer bowl combine 1½ cups *all-purpose flour* and 1 package *active dry yeast*. Heat 1½ cups shredded *American or Swiss cheese*, 1¼ cups *water*, ¼ cup *sugar*, and 1½ teaspoons *salt* just till warm (115° to 120°), stirring constantly. Add to flour mixture; add 1 *egg*. Beat at low speed of electric mixer for ½ minute, scraping bowl. Beat 3 minutes at high speed. Stir in as much of 2 to 2½ cups *all-purpose flour* as you can mix in with a spoon. On a floured surface knead in enough of the remaining all-purpose flour to make a moderately stiff dough that is smooth and elastic (6 to 8 minutes total). Shape into a ball in a greased bowl; turn once. Cover; let rise in a warm place till double (1 to 1¼ hours).

Punch down; divide in half. Cover; let rest 10 minutes. Shape into 2 loaves; place in greased 8×4×2-inch loaf pans. Cover; let rise till nearly double (about 45 minutes). Bake in a 350° oven 40 to 45 minutes. Cover with foil the last 20 minutes to prevent overbrowning. Cool on a wire rack. Makes 2 loaves.

KUCHEN

 3 cups all-purpose flour
 1 package active dry yeast
 ¾ cup milk
 6 tablespoons butter or margarine
 ⅓ cup sugar
 ½ teaspoon salt
 2 eggs
 1 beaten egg
 3 tablespoons light cream or milk
 1 cup sugar
 1½ teaspoons ground cinnamon
 2 cups thinly sliced peeled apple, sliced rhubarb, sliced Italian plums, or cottage cheese

Oven 400°

In a mixer bowl combine *1½ cups* of the flour and the yeast. In a saucepan heat ¾ cup milk, butter, ⅓ cup sugar, and salt just till warm (115° to 120°) and butter is almost melted, stirring constantly. Add to flour mixture; add 2 eggs. Beat at low speed of electric mixer ½ minute, scraping bowl. Beat 3 minutes at high speed. Stir in remaining flour. Divide in half. With lightly floured fingers, pat into two greased 9×1½-inch round baking pans, pressing up sides to form a rim. Cover; let rise in a warm place till double (45 to 50 minutes).

Combine the beaten egg and 3 tablespoons cream or milk. Stir in 1 cup sugar and the cinnamon. (If cottage cheese is used, stir into the sugar-cream mixture.) Arrange fruit atop risen dough. Carefully spoon sugar-cream mixture over fruit. Bake in a 400° oven for 20 to 25 minutes. Cool slightly. Cut into wedges; serve warm. Makes 2 coffee cakes.

ANADAMA BREAD

6¼ to 6¾ cups all-purpose flour
½ cup cornmeal
2 packages active dry yeast
½ cup dark molasses
⅓ cup shortening
2 eggs   Oven 375°

Combine *3 cups* flour, cornmeal, and the yeast. Heat molasses, shortening, 2 cups *water*, and 1 tablespoon *salt* just till warm (115° to 120°); stir constantly. Add to flour mixture; add eggs. Beat at low speed of electric mixer ½ minute. Beat 3 minutes at high speed. Stir in as much remaining flour as you can mix in with a spoon. On a floured surface knead in enough remaining flour to make a moderately soft dough (3 to 5 minutes total). Shape into a ball in a greased bowl; turn once. Cover; let rise in a warm place till double (1 to 1¼ hours). Punch down; divide in half. Cover; let rest 10 minutes. Grease two 9×5×3-inch loaf pans. Shape dough into 2 loaves; place in pans. Cover; let rise till nearly double (45 to 60 minutes). Bake in a 375° oven 35 to 40 minutes. Makes 2.

Quick Breads

It's easy to understand why quick breads are so popular. First of all, there's such a wide variety of taste-tempting breads from which to choose. And, they're relatively speedy to prepare and bake, especially when you take into account the rising time necessary for yeast bread preparation.

The following are quick bread tips and explanations.

Baking powder, baking soda, steam, or air—rather than yeast—leaven quick breads.

Most quick breads are best served hot from the oven—with plenty of butter!

Most nut breads should be stored for at least a day. The flavors will mellow and the loaf will slice more easily.

After baking, turn nut breads out of the pan and cool on a wire rack. Place cooled bread in an airtight container, or wrap it in foil or clear plastic wrap.

A crack down the center of a nut loaf is no mistake—it's typical.

Serve nut breads cut in very thin slices with simple spreads: soft butter, cream cheese, jam, or jelly.

Dip tops of warm muffins in melted butter or margarine and then in sugar for a sweet and sparkling crusty topping.

BASIC MUFFINS

1¾ cups all-purpose flour
¼ cup sugar
2½ teaspoons baking powder
¾ teaspoon salt
1 beaten egg
¾ cup milk
⅓ cup cooking oil   Oven 400°

In a large mixing bowl stir together the flour, sugar, baking powder, and salt. Make a well in the center. Combine egg, milk, and oil. Add egg mixture all at once to flour mixture. Stir just till moistened; batter should be lumpy. Grease muffin cups or line with paper bake cups; fill ⅔ full. Bake in a 400° oven for 20 to 25 minutes or till golden. Remove from pans; serve warm. Makes 10 to 12 muffins.

Cranberry Muffins: Prepare Basic Muffins as at left, *except* coarsely chop 1 cup fresh or frozen *cranberries* and combine with ¼ cup additional *sugar*. Fold into batter.

Apple-Raisin Muffins: Prepare Basic Muffins as at left, *except* stir ½ teaspoon ground *cinnamon* into the flour mixture. Fold 1 cup chopped peeled *apple* and ¼ cup *raisins* into batter.

Banana-Nut Muffins: Prepare Basic Muffins as at left, *except* decrease milk to ½ *cup*. Stir in 1 cup mashed *banana* and ½ cup chopped *nuts* into batter.

POPOVERS

1½ teaspoons shortening
2 beaten eggs
1 cup milk
1 tablespoon cooking oil
1 cup all-purpose flour   Oven 450°

Grease six 6-ounce custard cups with ¼ *teaspoon* of the shortening for *each* cup. Place custard cups on a 15 × 10 × 1-inch baking pan or baking sheet and place in oven; preheat oven to 450°. Meanwhile, in a 4-cup liquid measure or mixing bowl combine beaten eggs, milk, and oil. Add flour and ½ teaspoon *salt*. Beat with electric mixer or rotary beater till mixture is smooth. Remove pan from oven. Fill the hot custard cups *half* full. Return to oven. Bake in a 450° oven for 20 minutes. Reduce oven to 350°; bake 15 to 20 minutes more or till *very firm*. (If popovers brown too quickly, turn off oven and finish baking in the cooling oven till very firm.) A few minutes before removing from oven, prick each popover with a fork to let steam escape. Serve hot. Makes 6.

THREE-C BREAD

2½ cups all-purpose flour
1 cup sugar
1 teaspoon baking powder
1 teaspoon baking soda
½ teaspoon ground mace
3 beaten eggs
½ cup cooking oil
½ cup milk
2 cups shredded carrots
1⅓ cups flaked coconut
½ cup chopped maraschino cherries Oven 350°

Stir together flour, sugar, baking powder, soda, mace, and ½ teaspoon *salt*. Combine eggs, oil, and milk. Add to dry ingredients; mix well. Stir in carrots, coconut, and cherries. Pour into 3 greased 21-ounce pie filling cans. Bake in a 350° oven for 1 to 1½ hours. (Or, pour batter into one greased 9×5×3-inch loaf pan. Bake in a 350° oven 45 to 50 minutes.) Cool in cans 10 minutes. Remove from cans; cool completely. Wrap and store overnight before slicing. Makes 3.

NUT BREAD

3 cups all-purpose flour
1 cup sugar
4 teaspoons baking powder
1 teaspoon salt
1 beaten egg
1⅔ cups milk
¼ cup cooking oil
¾ cup chopped nuts   Oven 350°

Stir together the flour, sugar, baking powder, and salt. Combine egg, milk, and oil; add to dry ingredients, stirring just till combined. Stir in nuts. Turn into a greased 9 × 5 × 3-inch loaf pan. Bake in a 350° oven about 1 to 1¼ hours. Cool in pan 10 minutes. Remove from pan; cool on a rack. Wrap and store overnight before slicing. Makes 1.

Cheese-Nut Bread: Prepare Nut Bread as above, *except* add 1 cup shredded *cheese* (4 ounces) to batter with nuts.

ZUCCHINI NUT LOAF

- 1½ cups all-purpose flour
- 1 teaspoon ground cinnamon
- ½ teaspoon baking soda
- ½ teaspoon salt
- ½ teaspoon ground nutmeg
- ¼ teaspoon baking powder
- 1 cup sugar
- 1 cup finely shredded unpeeled zucchini
- 1 egg
- ¼ cup cooking oil
- ¼ teaspoon finely shredded lemon peel
- ½ cup chopped walnuts   Oven 350°

In a mixing bowl stir together flour, cinnamon, baking soda, salt, nutmeg, and baking powder; set aside. In a mixing bowl beat together sugar, shredded zucchini, and egg. Add oil and lemon peel; mix well. Stir flour mixture into zucchini mixture. Gently fold in chopped nuts. Turn batter into a greased 8 × 4 × 2-inch loaf pan. Bake in 350° oven for 55 to 60 minutes or till a wooden pick inserted near center comes out clean. Cool in pan 10 minutes. Remove from pan; cool thoroughly on a rack. Wrap and store loaf overnight before slicing. Makes 1.

BOSTON BROWN BREAD

In a mixing bowl stir together ½ cup *whole wheat flour*, ¼ cup *all-purpose flour*, ¼ cup *yellow cornmeal*, ½ teaspoon *baking powder*, ¼ teaspoon *baking soda*, and ¼ teaspoon *salt*. In another mixing bowl combine 1 *egg*, ¼ cup *light molasses*, 2 tablespoons *sugar*, and 2 teaspoons *cooking oil*. Add flour mixture and ¾ cup *buttermilk or sour milk* alternately to the molasses mixture; beat well. Stir in ¼ cup *raisins*.

Turn batter into two well-greased 16-ounce vegetable cans. Cover cans tightly with foil. Place cans on a rack set in a large Dutch oven. Pour hot water into Dutch oven to a depth of 1 inch. Bring to boiling; reduce heat. Cover; simmer 2½ to 3 hours or till done. Add boiling water as needed. Remove cans from pan; let stand 10 minutes. Remove bread from cans. Serve warm. Makes 2.

SPICY BUTTERMILK COFFEE CAKE

- 2½ cups all-purpose flour
- 2 cups packed brown sugar
- ⅔ cup shortening
- 2 teaspoons baking powder
- ½ teaspoon baking soda
- ½ teaspoon ground cinnamon
- ½ teaspoon ground nutmeg
- 1 cup buttermilk or sour milk
- 2 beaten eggs
- ⅓ cup chopped nuts

Oven 375°

Combine flour, brown sugar, and ½ teaspoon *salt*. Cut in shortening till mixture is crumbly; set aside ½ *cup* crumb mixture. To remaining crumb mixture add baking powder, soda, and spices; mix well. Add buttermilk or sour milk and eggs; mix well. Pour into two greased

> **Making Sour Milk**
> When you don't have any buttermilk on hand, substitute an equal amount of "soured" milk for the buttermilk. To make sour milk, combine 1 tablespoon *lemon juice or vinegar* and enough whole *milk* to make *1 cup* total liquid. Let the mixture stand 5 minutes before using in the recipe.

8×1½-inch or 9×1½-inch round baking pans. Combine reserved crumbs with nuts; sprinkle atop cakes. Bake in a 375° oven for 20 to 25 minutes. Serve warm. Makes 2 coffee cakes.

STREUSEL COFFEE CAKE

- **1½ cups all-purpose flour**
- **¾ cup granulated sugar**
- **2 teaspoons baking powder**
- **½ teaspoon salt**
- **1 beaten egg**
- **½ cup milk**
- **¼ cup cooking oil**
- **½ cup raisins**
- **½ cup chopped nuts**
- **¼ cup packed brown sugar**
- **1 tablespoon all-purpose flour**
- **1 tablespoon butter or margarine, softened**
- **1 teaspoon ground cinnamon**   Oven 375°

Stir together the 1½ cups flour, granulated sugar, baking powder, and salt. Combine egg, milk, and oil. Add to flour mixture; mix well. Stir in raisins. Turn into a greased 9×9×2-inch baking pan. Combine nuts, brown sugar, 1 tablespoon flour, butter or margarine, and cinnamon; sprinkle over batter. Bake in a 375° oven about 25 minutes. Makes 1 coffee cake.

CHERRY-PECAN BREAD

Oven 350°

In a mixing bowl thoroughly stir together 2 cups *all-purpose flour*, 1 teaspoon *baking soda*, and ½ teaspoon *salt*; set aside. In a large mixer bowl beat together ¾ cup *sugar*, ½ cup *butter or margarine*, 2 *eggs*, and 1 teaspoon *vanilla* till light and fluffy. Add flour mixture and 1 cup *buttermilk or sour milk* alternately to beaten mixture. Beat just till blended after each addition. Fold in 1 cup chopped *pecans* and 1 cup chopped *maraschino cherries*. Turn batter into a lightly greased 9×5×3-inch loaf pan. Bake in a 350° oven for 55 to 60 minutes. Cool in pan 10 minutes. Remove from pan; cool. If desired, glaze with Powdered Sugar Icing. Makes 1 loaf.

Powdered Sugar Icing: Combine 1 cup sifted *powdered sugar*, ¼ teaspoon *vanilla*, and enough *milk* for drizzling.

APPLE FRITTER RINGS

Core and peel 4 large tart cooking *apples*; cut into ½-inch-thick rings and set aside. In a mixing bowl thoroughly stir together 1 cup *all-purpose flour*, 2 tablespoons *sugar*, 1 teaspoon *baking powder*, and dash *salt*. Combine 1 beaten *egg*, ⅔ cup *milk*, and 1 teaspoon *cooking oil*; add all at once to flour mixture, stirring just till combined.

In a skillet that is at least 2 inches deep, heat 1 inch *shortening or cooking oil* to 375°. Dip apple slices in batter one at a time. Fry fritters in hot fat about 1½ minutes per side or till golden brown, turning once. Drain on paper toweling. Sprinkle hot fritters with a mixture of ¼ cup *sugar* and ½ teaspoon ground *cinnamon*. Serve hot. Makes 16 fritters.

CAKES

Cakes are grouped into three classes; those made with shortening (conventional and quick-mix), those made without shortening (angel and sponge), and combination angel and shortening types (chiffon).

For a shortening-type cake, grease and lightly flour bottoms of pans, or line bottoms with waxed paper. Pans for angel, sponge, and chiffon cakes should not be greased, unless specified.

A shortening-type cake is done when a cake tester or wooden pick inserted in the center comes out clean. The cake also will shrink slightly from the sides of the pan. Angel, sponge, and chiffon cakes are done when the cake springs back when touched lightly with your finger.

Cool shortening layer cakes in their pans on wire racks 10 minutes (loaf cakes, 15 minutes), then loosen edges. Place an inverted rack on the cake and turn all over; carefully lift off the pan. Put a second rack over the cake and invert again so the top side is up. Invert angel, sponge, and chiffon cakes in their pans as they are removed from the oven to prevent them from shrinking or falling.

BUSY-DAY CAKE

1½ cups all-purpose flour
¾ cup sugar
2½ teaspoons baking powder
¾ cup milk
⅓ cup shortening
1 egg
1½ teaspoons vanilla   Oven 375°

Grease and lightly flour a 9×9×2-inch baking pan. In a small mixer bowl combine all ingredients and ½ teaspoon *salt*. Beat with electric mixer till combined. Beat 2 minutes on medium speed. Turn into pan. Bake in a 375° oven 25 to 30 minutes or till done. Cool. Serves 9.

CARROT CAKE

2 cups all-purpose flour
2 cups sugar
1 teaspoon baking powder
1 teaspoon baking soda
1 teaspoon salt
1 teaspoon ground cinnamon
3 cups finely shredded carrot
1 cup cooking oil
4 eggs
Cream Cheese Frosting (see recipe, page 47)
                                        Oven 325°

Grease and lightly flour a 13×9×2-inch baking pan (or two 9×1½-inch round baking pans). In a mixer bowl combine the first 6 ingredients. Add next 3 ingredients, beating with electric mixer till combined. Beat on medium speed for 2 minutes. Turn into pan(s). Bake in a 325° oven for 50 to 60 minutes in the 13×9×2-inch pan or till done. (For two 9-inch layers, bake in a 325° oven for 40 minutes or till done.) Cool on a wire rack. (Remove layers from pans after cooling 10 minutes. Cool well.) Frost with Cream Cheese Frosting. Serves 12 to 15.

APPLESAUCE SPICE CAKE

- 2½ cups all-purpose flour
- 1½ teaspoons baking soda
- 1 teaspoon salt
- 1 teaspoon ground cinnamon
- ¾ teaspoon ground nutmeg
- ½ teaspoon ground cloves
- ¼ teaspoon baking powder
- ½ cup butter or margarine
- 2 cups sugar
- 2 eggs
- 1 16-ounce can applesauce
- ¾ cup raisins
- ½ cup chopped nuts   Oven 350°

Grease and lightly flour a 13×9×2-inch baking pan. Combine the first 7 ingredients. In a mixer bowl beat butter with electric mixer for 30 seconds. Add sugar and beat till well combined. Add eggs, one at a time, beating 1 minute after each. Add dry ingredients and applesauce alternately to beaten mixture, beating on low speed after each addition. Stir in raisins and nuts. Turn into pan. Bake in a 350° oven for 45 minutes or till done. Cool on a wire rack. Serves 12 to 15.

BUTTERSCOTCH MARBLE CAKE

- 1 package 2-layer-size white cake mix
- 1 4-serving-size package instant butterscotch pudding mix
- ¼ cup cooking oil
- 4 eggs
- ½ cup chocolate-flavored syrup
- ½ recipe Chocolate Icing (see recipe, page 47)

Oven 350°

Grease and lightly flour a 10-inch fluted tube pan. In a large mixer bowl combine cake mix, pudding mix, oil, eggs, and 1 cup *water*. Beat at low speed of electric mixer till combined, then at medium speed for 2 minutes. Reserve 1½ cups batter. Turn remaining batter into pan. Stir together reserved batter and the chocolate syrup. Pour chocolate mixture atop butterscotch batter. Swirl with a metal spatula or spoon to marble. Bake in a 350° oven about 60 minutes or till done. Cool 15 minutes on a wire rack. Invert onto rack; remove pan. Cool. Glaze with Chocolate Icing. Serves 12.

FEATHERY FUDGE CAKE

- 2 cups all-purpose flour
- 1¼ teaspoons baking soda
- ½ teaspoon salt
- ⅔ cup butter or margarine
- 1¾ cups sugar
- 1 teaspoon vanilla
- 2 eggs
- 3 squares (3 ounces) unsweetened chocolate, melted and cooled
- 1¼ cups cold water

Oven 350°

Grease and lightly flour two 9×1½-inch round baking pans. Combine the first 3 ingredients. In a mixer bowl beat butter on medium speed of electric mixer about 30 seconds. Add sugar and vanilla and beat till well combined. Add eggs, one at a time, beating 1 minute after each. Beat in cooled chocolate. Add dry ingredients and cold water alternately to beaten mixture, beating after each addition. Turn into pans. Bake in a 350° oven for 30 to 35 minutes or till done. Cool 10 minutes on wire racks. Remove from pans. Cool. Makes 12 servings.

GINGERBREAD

- 1½ cups all-purpose flour
- ¾ teaspoon ground ginger
- ¾ teaspoon ground cinnamon
- ½ teaspoon baking powder
- ½ teaspoon baking soda
- ½ teaspoon salt
- ½ cup shortening
- ¼ cup packed brown sugar
- 1 egg
- ½ cup light molasses
- ½ cup boiling water   Oven 350°

Grease and lightly flour a 9×1½-inch round baking pan. Combine the first 6 ingredients. In a mixer bowl beat shortening on medium speed of electric mixer about 30 seconds. Add brown sugar; beat till fluffy. Add egg and molasses; beat 1 minute. Add dry ingredients and water alternately to beaten mixture, beating after each addition. Turn into prepared pan. Bake in a 350° oven 30 to 35 minutes or till done. Cool 10 minutes on a wire rack. Remove from pan; serve warm. Makes 8 servings.

GERMAN CHOCOLATE CAKE

- 1 4-ounce package German sweet chocolate
- 1⅔ cups all-purpose flour
- 1 teaspoon baking soda
- ½ cup butter or margarine
- 1 cup sugar
- 1 teaspoon vanilla
- 3 egg yolks
- ⅔ cup buttermilk or sour milk
- 3 stiff-beaten egg whites
- Coconut-Pecan Frosting (see recipe, page 48)

Oven 350°

Grease and lightly flour two 8 × 1½-inch round baking pans. Heat chocolate and ⅓ cup *water* till chocolate melts; cool. Combine flour, soda, and ½ teaspoon *salt*. Beat butter about 30 seconds. Add sugar and vanilla; beat till fluffy. Add egg yolks, one at a time, beating 1 minute after each. Beat in chocolate mixture. Add dry ingredients and buttermilk alternately to beaten mixture, beating after each addition. Fold in egg whites. Turn into pans. Bake in a 350° oven for 30 to 35 minutes. Cool 10 minutes. Remove from pans; cool. Fill and frost top with Coconut-Pecan Frosting. Serves 12.

ANGEL CAKE

- 1½ cups sifted powdered sugar
- 1 cup sifted cake flour or sifted all-purpose flour
- 1½ cups egg whites (11 or 12 large)
- 1½ teaspoons cream of tartar
- 1 teaspoon vanilla
- 1 cup granulated sugar

Oven 350°

Sift together powdered sugar and cake or all-purpose flour; repeat sifting twice. In a large mixer bowl beat egg whites, cream of tartar, vanilla, and ¼ teaspoon *salt* at medium speed of electric mixer till soft peaks form. Gradually add granulated sugar, about 2 tablespoons at a time. Continue beating till stiff peaks form. Sift about ¼ of the flour mixture over whites; fold in lightly by hand. If bowl is too full, transfer to a larger bowl. Repeat, folding in remaining flour mixture by fourths. Turn into an *ungreased* 10-inch tube pan. Bake on lowest rack in a 350° oven about 40 minutes or till done. Invert cake in pan; cool completely. Loosen cake from pan; remove. Serves 12.

HOT MILK SPONGE CAKE

- 1 cup all-purpose flour
- 1 teaspoon baking powder
- 2 eggs
- 1 cup sugar
- ½ cup milk
- 2 tablespoons butter or margarine
- Broiled Coconut Topping (see recipe, page 48)

Oven 350°

Grease a 9×9×2-inch baking pan. Combine flour, baking powder, and ¼ teaspoon *salt*. In a small mixer bowl beat eggs at high speed 4 minutes or till thick. Gradually add sugar; beat at medium speed 4 to 5 minutes or till sugar dissolves. Add dry ingredients to egg mixture; stir just till combined. Heat milk with butter till butter melts; stir into batter and mix well. Turn into pan. Bake in a 350° oven for 20 to 25 minutes. Frost while warm with Broiled Coconut Topping. Serve warm. Serves 9.

GOLDEN CHIFFON CAKE

  7 eggs
2¼ cups sifted cake flour or 2 cups all-purpose flour
1½ cups sugar
  1 tablespoon baking powder
 ½ cup cooking oil
  2 teaspoons grated lemon peel
  1 teaspoon vanilla
 ½ teaspoon cream of tartar   Oven 325°

Separate egg yolks from whites. In a large mixer bowl sift together cake or all-purpose flour, sugar, baking powder, and 1 teaspoon *salt*; make a well in the center. Add oil, egg yolks, peel, vanilla, and ¾ cup cold *water*. Beat at low speed of electric mixer till combined, then on high speed about 5 minutes or till satin smooth. Thoroughly wash beaters. In a large mixing bowl combine egg whites and cream of tartar; beat till stiff peaks form. Pour batter in a thin stream over surface of egg whites; fold in gently by hand. Pour into an *ungreased* 10-inch tube pan. Bake in a 325° oven 65 to 70 minutes. Invert; cool completely. Loosen cake from pan; remove. Serves 12.

Frostings

FLUFFY WHITE FROSTING

1 cup sugar
¼ teaspoon cream of tartar
2 egg whites
1 teaspoon vanilla

In a saucepan combine sugar, cream of tartar, ⅓ cup *water*, and dash *salt*. Cook and stir till bubbly and sugar dissolves. In a mixer bowl combine egg whites and vanilla. Add sugar syrup very slowly to unbeaten egg whites while beating constantly at high speed of electric mixer about 7 minutes or till stiff peaks form. Frost tops and sides of two 8- or 9-inch layers or one 10-inch tube cake.

CHOCOLATE ICING

- **1 4-ounce package German sweet chocolate, broken up**
- **3 tablespoons butter or margarine**
- **1½ cups sifted powdered sugar**

In a small saucepan melt together the chocolate and butter over low heat. Remove from heat; stir in powdered sugar and 3 tablespoons *hot water*. Add more hot water, if needed, to make of pouring consistency. Spoon over cake. Glazes top of a 10-inch tube cake.

CREAM CHEESE FROSTING

- **1 3-ounce package cream cheese**
- **¼ cup butter or margarine**
- **1 teaspoon vanilla**
- **2 cups sifted powdered sugar**

In a mixer bowl beat together cream cheese, butter or margarine, and vanilla till light and fluffy. Gradually add powdered sugar, beating till smooth. Spread over cooled cake; sprinkle with chopped nuts, if desired. Frosts tops of two 8- or 9-inch layers. Cover; store in the refrigerator.

COCONUT-PECAN FROSTING

> 1 egg
> 1 5⅓-ounce can (⅔ cup) evaporated milk
> ⅔ cup sugar
> ¼ cup butter or margarine
> Dash salt
> 1⅓ cups flaked coconut
> ½ cup chopped pecans

In a saucepan beat egg slightly. Stir in milk, sugar, butter or margarine, and salt. Cook and stir over medium heat about 12 minutes or till thickened and bubbly. Stir in coconut and pecans. Cool thoroughly. Spread on cake. Frosts top of one 13×9-inch cake or tops of two 8- or 9-inch layers.

BROILED COCONUT TOPPING

> ½ cup packed brown sugar
> 3 tablespoons butter or margarine, softened
> 2 tablespoons milk
> 1 cup flaked coconut

In a mixer bowl beat brown sugar and butter or margarine till fluffy. Stir in milk. Stir in coconut; spread over warm cake in pan. Broil 4 inches from heat 3 to 4 minutes or till golden. Serve warm. Frosts top of a 9×9-inch cake. (Double recipe for top of one 13×9-inch cake.)

CANDY

The secret of making good candy is to follow recipe directions exactly. And the secret of keeping candy at its best is to store it properly.

Fudge and fondant will stay fresh and creamy for several weeks if tightly wrapped in waxed paper, foil, or clear plastic wrap. Store the wrapped candy in an airtight container in a cool, dry place.

EASY FUDGE

- ½ cup butter or margarine
- ⅓ cup water
- 1 16-ounce package powdered sugar
- ½ cup nonfat dry milk powder
- ½ cup unsweetened cocoa powder
- Dash salt
- ½ cup chopped nuts

In a small saucepan heat together butter or margarine and water just to boiling, stirring to melt butter or margarine. Sift together powdered sugar, dry milk powder, cocoa powder, and salt into a large mixer bowl. (If powdered sugar mixture seems lumpy, sift again.) Add melted butter mixture. Stir till well blended; stir in chopped nuts. Turn into a buttered 8×8×2-inch pan. Chill several hours. Cut into squares. Makes about 1½ pounds.

CHOCO-SCOTCH CRUNCHIES

- 1 6-ounce package (1 cup) butterscotch pieces
- 1 6-ounce package (1 cup) semisweet chocolate pieces
- 1 3-ounce can (2½ cups) chow mein noodles
- 1 cup salted peanuts or cashews
- 1 cup tiny marshmallows

In a medium saucepan melt butterscotch and chocolate pieces over low heat, stirring occasionally. Remove from heat. Stir in chow mein noodles, nuts, and marshmallows. Drop from a teaspoon onto waxed paper. Refrigerate till firm. Makes 3 to 4 dozen.

Microwave directions: In a large nonmetal bowl combine butterscotch and chocolate pieces. Cook, uncovered, in a counter-top microwave oven on high power for about 2½ minutes or till melted. Stir after each minute. Stir in chow mein noodles, nuts, and marshmallows. Drop from a teaspoon onto waxed paper. Chill till firm.

CHOCOLATE NUT BALLS

- 1 6-ounce package (1 cup) semisweet chocolate pieces
- 2 tablespoons butter or margarine
- 1 egg
- 1 cup sifted powdered sugar
- ½ teaspoon vanilla
  Dash salt
- ½ cup flaked coconut
- ½ cup chopped peanuts
  Flaked coconut

In a medium saucepan melt semisweet chocolate pieces and butter or margarine over low heat, stirring frequently. Remove pan from heat; cool to lukewarm.

Beat in egg till smooth and glossy. Add sifted powdered sugar, vanilla, and salt; mix well. Stir in the ½ cup flaked coconut and the chopped peanuts. Chill about 1 hour. Form into 1-inch balls; roll in additional flaked coconut. Arrange on a baking sheet. Chill at least 3 hours or till firm. Makes about 2½ dozen balls.

CREAM CHEESE MINTS

These mints can be frozen for up to 1 month—
- 1 3-ounce package cream cheese, softened
- ½ teaspoon peppermint extract
- 3 cups sifted powdered sugar
- Few drops food coloring
- Granulated sugar

In a small mixer bowl combine softened cream cheese and peppermint extract. Gradually beat in powdered sugar with electric mixer till mixture is smooth. (Knead in the last of the powdered sugar with your hands.) Knead in food coloring till evenly distributed.

Sprinkle small candy molds lightly with granulated sugar. Press about ½ to ¾ *teaspoon* cream cheese mixture into each mold. Remove from mold. (*Or*, form mixture into ¾-inch balls. Dip each ball in granulated sugar, place on waxed paper. Flatten each with the bottom of a juice glass or with the tines of a fork.) Let dry overnight. Makes 6 to 8 dozen molded mints or about 4 dozen patties.

PEPPERMINT BONBONS

- 1 pound confectioners' coating for dipping
- ½ cup whipping cream
- 1¼ teaspoon peppermint extract
- Crushed peppermint candies

In a heavy 2-quart saucepan melt confectioners' coating over low heat, stirring frequently. Remove from heat. Stir in whipping cream and peppermint extract. Beat at high speed of electric mixer till smooth. Chill in *freezer* for 20 to 30 minutes or till candy is stiff enough to be shaped.

Form candy into balls, using 2 teaspoons candy for each ball. Roll balls in crushed peppermint candies. Arrange on a baking sheet. Store in refrigerator. Makes 3½ dozen.

EASY WALNUT PENUCHE

- 6 tablespoons butter or margarine
- 1 cup packed brown sugar
- ¼ cup milk
- 2½ cups sifted powdered sugar
- 1 cup chopped walnuts

In a 1½-quart saucepan melt butter or margarine; add brown sugar. Cook over low heat for 2 minutes; stir constantly. Increase heat to medium; add milk. Cook and stir till mixture boils. Remove from heat; cool 30 minutes. Gradually stir in powdered sugar till mixture is of fudge consistency. Stir in nuts. Spread in a buttered 9×5×3-inch or 8×4×2-inch loaf pan. Chill. Cut into squares. Makes 1½ pounds.

COOKIES

Bar Cookies: Test cakelike bars for doneness with a wooden pick. Fudgelike bars are done when a slight imprint remains after touching lightly. Cool bar cookies before frosting unless otherwise specified. The yield of bar cookies depends on the size of the pan as well as the size of the serving. Generally, thicker and richer bars should be cut into smaller pieces. Bar cookies can be cut into diamond shapes by making diagonal cuts in one direction and cuts straight across in the other direction.

Drop Cookies: When dropping dough on a cookie sheet, allow ample room for cookies to spread during baking. Prevent excessive spreading of cookies by chilling dough, dropping onto a cooled cookie sheet, baking at the correct temperature, and mounding dough when dropping it. Cool baked cookies on wire racks. When storing, do not mix soft and crisp varieties in the same container, or the crisp types will become soft.

Shaped Cookies: Cookie dough can be flattened with the bottom of a glass that has been dipped in sugar, with the tines of a fork, or with your thumb, or certain dough can be shaped by putting it through a cookie press. For best results with a cookie press, keep the dough pliable to obtain well-defined patterns.

Rolled and Refrigerated Cookies: For rolled cookies, roll a small amount of dough at a time, keeping the rest chilled. Use a pastry cloth and a stockinette cover for the rolling pin. Roll from center to edge as for piecrust. Using a lightly floured cutter, start cutting at the edge of dough and work toward the center. Be sure the dough is chilled; unchilled dough takes up too much flour, which causes cookies to be tough. Excessive rerolling of pieces of dough also causes toughness.

Chill dough for refrigerator cookies thoroughly before slicing. Use a sawing motion with a sharp knife when slicing cookies to retain shape. For extra crisp cookies, slice thin and bake till lightly browned.

Bar Cookies

APRICOT-FILLED OATMEAL BARS

- 1½ cups all-purpose flour
- 1½ cups quick-cooking rolled oats
- 1 cup packed brown sugar
- ½ teaspoon baking soda
- ¾ cup butter or margarine
- 1 cup apricot preserves

Oven 375°

Stir together flour, oats, brown sugar, and soda. Cut in butter till mixture is crumbly. Pat ⅔ of the crumbs in the bottom of an ungreased 13×9×2-inch baking pan; spread with preserves. Sprinkle with remaining crumbs. Bake in a 375° oven for 25 to 30 minutes. Cool on a wire rack. Cut into bars. Makes 30.

Prune-Filled Oatmeal Bars: Prepare Apricot-Filled Oatmeal Bars as above, *except* omit apricot preserves and use prune filling. For prune filling, in a saucepan combine 1 cup snipped, pitted *prunes*, ⅔ cup *water*, and ½ of a 6-ounce can (⅓ cup) *lemonade concentrate*.

Cover; simmer 5 minutes. Mix ½ cup packed *brown sugar*, ½ cup chopped *walnuts*, and 2 tablespoons all-purpose *flour*; stir into prune mixture. Cook and stir till very thick. Spread atop crumb mixture. Continue as directed.

CHOCOLATE-CREAM CHEESE BROWNIES

- 1 6-ounce package (1 cup) semisweet chocolate pieces
- 2 tablespoons butter or margarine
- ½ cup all-purpose flour
- ½ teaspoon baking powder
- 2 eggs
- 1½ teaspoons vanilla
- 1 cup sugar
- ½ cup chopped walnuts
- 1 3-ounce package cream cheese, softened
- 1 beaten egg   Oven 350°

Grease and lightly flour an 8×8×2-inch baking pan. Melt chocolate and butter; cool. Stir together flour, baking powder, and ¼ teaspoon *salt*. In a mixer bowl beat 2 eggs and *1 teaspoon* of the vanilla; gradually add ¾ *cup* of the sugar. Continue beating eggs till thick and lemon colored. Add dry ingredients to egg mixture; beat till well combined. Stir in chocolate mixture; stir in nuts. Beat cheese and remaining ¼ cup sugar till fluffy. Stir in remaining egg and ½ teaspoon vanilla. Spread *half* of the chocolate mixture in pan. Pour cheese mixture over; top with remaining chocolate mixture. Swirl layers to marble, if desired. Bake in a 350° oven about 45 minutes. Cool on a wire rack. Cut into bars. Makes 16.

BLONDE BROWNIES

2 cups all-purpose flour
2 teaspoons baking powder
½ cup butter or margarine
2 cups packed brown sugar
2 eggs
1 teaspoon vanilla
1 cup chopped walnuts   Oven 350°

Grease a 13×9×2-inch baking pan. Combine flour, baking powder, and ¼ teaspoon *salt*. Melt butter; remove from heat. Stir in sugar. Add eggs and vanilla; stir till combined. Stir dry ingredients and walnuts into sugar mixture. Spread in pan. Bake in a 350° oven 20 to 25 minutes. Cut into bars while warm. Makes 48.

SEVEN-LAYER BARS

½ cup butter or margarine
1½ cups finely crushed graham crackers
1 6-ounce package (1 cup) semisweet
   chocolate pieces
1 6-ounce package (1 cup) butterscotch pieces
1 3½-ounce can (1⅓ cups) flaked coconut
½ cup chopped walnuts
1 14-ounce can (1⅓ cups) sweetened
   condensed milk   Oven 350°

Melt butter; stir in crushed graham crackers. Pat crumb mixture evenly in bottom of an ungreased 13×9×2-inch baking pan. Layer, in order, chocolate pieces, butterscotch pieces, coconut, and walnuts. Pour sweetened condensed milk evenly over all. Bake in a 350° oven 30 minutes; cool. Cut into bars. Makes 36.

Drop Cookies

BASIC DROP COOKIES

1¼ cups all-purpose flour
½ teaspoon baking soda
¼ cup butter or margarine
¼ cup shortening
½ cup granulated sugar
¼ cup packed brown sugar
1 egg
1 teaspoon vanilla   Oven 375°

Grease a cookie sheet. Combine flour, soda, and ½ teaspoon *salt*. Beat butter and shortening with electric mixer for 30 seconds. Add sugars and beat till fluffy. Add egg and vanilla; beat well. Add dry ingredients to beaten mixture; beat well. Drop from a teaspoon 2 inches apart onto a greased cookie sheet. Bake in a 375° oven for 8 to 10 minutes. Remove; cool on a wire rack. Makes 30 to 36.

Lemon-Yogurt Cookies: Prepare Basic Drop Cookie dough as above, *except* stir in ½ cup *lemon yogurt* and ½ cup chopped toasted *almonds*. Bake as directed. Cool about 1 minute before removing to a wire rack. When cool, frost with a mixture of 2 cups sifted *powdered sugar* and ¼ cup *lemon yogurt*. Makes 36.

Chocolate-Peanut Cookies: Prepare Basic Drop Cookie dough as above, *except* use *1 cup* all-purpose flour and add 3 tablespoons *milk* to beaten mixture. Stir in 1½ squares (1½ ounces) *unsweetened chocolate*, melted and cooled, and ½ cup chopped *peanuts*. Bake as directed. Makes 40.

Pineapple-Coconut Drops: Prepare Basic Drop Cookie dough as above, *except* stir ¼ teaspoon ground *ginger* into dry ingredients. Stir in 1 cup *coconut*, ½ cup well-drained crushed *pineapple*, and ½ cup chopped *nuts*. Bake as directed. Makes 36 to 40.

Spicy Oatmeal-Raisin Cookies: Prepare Basic Drop Cookie dough as above, *except* use *1 cup* all-purpose flour, ½ teaspoon each ground *cinnamon* and *nutmeg*, and add 2 tablespoons *milk* to beaten mixture. Stir in 1 cup quick-cooking *rolled oats*, ½ cup *raisins*, and ½ cup chopped *nuts*. Bake as directed. Makes 40.

LEMON TEA COOKIES

    2 teaspoons lemon juice
    ½ cup milk
    1¾ cups all-purpose flour
    1 teaspoon baking powder
    ¼ teaspoon baking soda
    ½ cup butter or margarine
    ¾ cup sugar
    1 egg
    1 teaspoon finely shredded lemon peel
    Lemon Glaze   Oven 350°

Stir 2 teaspoons lemon juice into milk; set aside. Stir together flour, baking powder, soda, and ¼ teaspoon *salt*. Beat butter for 30 seconds; add sugar and beat till fluffy. Add egg and lemon peel; beat well. Add dry ingredients and milk mixture alternately to beaten mixture, beating well after each addition. Drop from a teaspoon 2 inches apart onto an ungreased cookie sheet. Bake in a 350° oven 12 to 14 minutes. Remove at once to a wire rack; brush Lemon Glaze over. Makes 48.

Lemon Glaze: Stir together ¾ cup *sugar* and ¼ cup *lemon juice*.

COCONUT MACAROONS

- 2 egg whites
- ½ teaspoon vanilla
- Dash salt
- ⅔ cup sugar
- 1 3½-ounce can (1⅓ cups) flaked coconut

Oven 325°

Grease a cookie sheet. Beat egg whites, vanilla, and salt till soft peaks form. Gradually add sugar, beating until stiff peaks form. Fold in coconut. Drop from a teaspoon 1½ inches apart onto a greased cookie sheet. Bake in a 325° oven about 20 minutes. Cool on a wire rack. Makes 20 to 24.

Shaped Cookies

ALMOND COOKIES

Oven 325°

Stir together 2¾ cups all-purpose *flour*, 1 cup *sugar*, ½ teaspoon *baking soda*, and ½ teaspoon *salt*. Cut in 1 cup *lard* till mixture resembles cornmeal. Combine 1 slightly beaten *egg*, 2 tablespoons *milk*, and 1 teaspoon *almond extract*; add to flour mixture. Mix well. Shape dough into 1-inch balls. Place 2 inches apart on an ungreased cookie sheet. Place a blanched *almond half* atop *each* cookie; press to flatten slightly. Bake in a 325° oven for 16 to 18 minutes. Cool on a wire rack. Makes 48.

SANDIES

  1 cup butter or margarine
  ⅓ cup granulated sugar
  2 teaspoons vanilla
  2 cups all-purpose flour
  1 cup chopped pecans
  ¼ cup powdered sugar   Oven 325°

Beat butter for 30 seconds; add granulated sugar and beat till fluffy. Add vanilla and 2 teaspoons *water*; beat well. Stir in flour and pecans. Shape into 1-inch balls or 1½ × ½-inch fingers. Place on an ungreased cookie sheet. Bake in a 325° oven about 20 minutes. Cool completely. Gently shake a few cookies at a time in a bag with powdered sugar. Makes 36.

GINGER CRINKLES

  2¼ cups all-purpose flour
  2 teaspoons baking soda
  1 teaspoon ground ginger
  1 teaspoon ground cinnamon
  ½ teaspoon ground cloves
  1 cup packed brown sugar
  ¾ cup shortening or cooking oil
  ¼ cup molasses
  1 egg   Oven 375°

Stir together the first 5 ingredients and ¼ teaspoon *salt*. Combine the remaining ingredients and beat well. Add dry ingredients to beaten mixture, beating well. Form 1-inch balls. Roll in granulated sugar, if desired; place 2 inches apart on ungreased cookie sheet. Bake in 375° oven about 10 minutes. Makes 48.

Rolled & Refrigerator Cookies

SANTA'S WHISKERS

1 cup butter or margarine
1 cup sugar
2 tablespoons milk
1 teaspoon vanilla
2½ cups all-purpose flour
1 cup finely chopped red or green candied cherries
½ cup finely chopped pecans
1 cup flaked coconut

Oven 375°

Beat butter for 30 seconds; add sugar and beat till fluffy. Add milk and vanilla; beat well. Stir in flour, then cherries and pecans. Shape into three 7-inch rolls. Roll dough in coconut to coat outside. Wrap in waxed paper or clear plastic wrap; chill thoroughly. Cut into ¼-inch slices. Place on an ungreased cookie sheet. Bake in a 375° oven 12 minutes or till edges are golden. Makes about 80.

CRISP PECAN DAINTIES

Oven 375°

Stir together 2⅓ cups all-purpose *flour*, 1 teaspoon *baking powder*, and ½ teaspoon *salt*. Beat ¾ cup *butter or margarine* for 30 seconds; add 1 cup *sugar* and beat till fluffy. Add 1 *egg*, 1 teaspoon finely shredded *lemon peel*, and 1 tablespoon *lemon juice*; beat well. Add dry ingredients to beaten mixture, beating till well combined. Stir in 1 cup finely chopped *pecans*. Shape dough into two 7-inch rolls. Wrap in waxed paper or clear plastic wrap; chill thoroughly. If sides flatten, roll on a flat surface to make round. Cut into ⅛-inch slices. Place on an ungreased cookie sheet. Bake in a 375° oven for 6 to 8 minutes. Cool on a wire rack. Makes about 78.

ROLLED GINGER COOKIES

    5 cups all-purpose flour
1½ teaspoons baking soda
    2 teaspoons ground ginger
    1 teaspoon ground cinnamon
    1 teaspoon ground cloves
    1 cup shortening
    1 cup sugar
    1 egg
    1 cup molasses
    2 tablespoons vinegar   Oven 375°

Grease a cookie sheet. Stir together flour, soda, spices, and ½ teaspoon *salt*. Beat shortening for 30 seconds. Add sugar; beat till fluffy. Add egg, molasses, and vinegar; beat well. Add dry ingredients to beaten mixture, beating well. Cover; chill 3 hours or overnight. Divide dough into thirds. On a lightly floured surface, roll *each* ⅓ of dough to ⅛-inch thickness. (Keep remainder chilled.) Cut into desired shapes. Place 1 inch apart on greased cookie sheet. Bake in a 375° oven for 5 to 6 minutes. Cool 1 minute; remove to a wire rack. Makes 60.

Note: Use the recipe above to make and cut out gingerbread men.

DESSERTS

Whether quick and simple or elegant and impressive, a dessert should end the meal on a delicious note. While it shouldn't dominate the food that precedes it, it shouldn't be lost or ignored, either. Remember, if you've served a hearty meal, a light dessert is in order; likewise, a more filling dessert provides a nice contrast to a lighter entrée. A simple fruit cup or pudding can be as appropriate as crepes served in a chafing dish.

Some desserts are best served warm, while others should be eaten chilled. Don't make the mistake of serving your dessert too hot or too cold, however. In fact, frozen desserts are best if allowed to stand at room temperature for a few minutes before they are served.

BREAD PUDDING

Oven 325°

Beat together 4 *eggs*, 2 cups *milk*, ⅓ cup *sugar*, ½ teaspoon ground *cinnamon*, ½ teaspoon *vanilla*, and ¼ teaspoon *salt*. Place 2½ cups *dry bread cubes* (3½ slices) in an 8×1½-inch round baking dish. Sprinkle ⅓ cup *raisins* over bread. Pour egg mixture over all. Bake in a 325° oven for 40 to 45 minutes or till a knife inserted near center comes out clean. Cool slightly. Makes 6 servings.

STIRRED CUSTARD

- 3 slightly beaten eggs
- 2 cups milk
- ¼ cup sugar
- Dash salt
- 1 teaspoon vanilla

In a heavy medium saucepan combine the eggs, milk, sugar, and salt. Cook and stir over medium heat. Continue cooking egg mixture till it coats a metal spoon. Remove from heat; cool at once by placing pan in a sink or bowl of ice water and stirring 1 to 2 minutes. Stir in vanilla. Pour custard mixture into a bowl. Cover surface with clear plastic wrap; chill till serving time. Makes 6 servings.

PRALINE CHEESE CUPS

- 1 4-ounce container whipped cream cheese
- ¼ cup dairy sour cream
- 2 tablespoons sugar
- ½ teaspoon vanilla
- 4 cake dessert cups
- ¼ cup pecan halves
- ½ cup caramel ice cream topping
- 1 tablespoon brandy

Combine cream cheese, sour cream, sugar, and vanilla. With a fork remove a small amount of the center from each dessert cup. Fill centers of dessert cups with cream cheese mixture. Arrange pecans atop each. Chill till serving time. Just before serving, in a saucepan heat together ice cream topping and brandy till warm. Spoon atop filled dessert cups. Makes 4 servings.

SAUCEPAN RICE PUDDING

 3 cups milk
 ½ cup long grain rice
 ⅓ cup raisins
 1 tablespoon butter or margarine
 ¼ cup sugar
 ¼ teaspoon ground cinnamon

In a heavy medium saucepan bring milk to boiling; stir in *uncooked* rice, raisins, and ¼ teaspoon *salt*. Cover; cook over low heat, stirring occasionally, for 30 to 40 minutes or till most of the milk is absorbed. (Mixture may appear curdled.) Spoon into dessert dishes. Dot with butter and sprinkle with a mixture of the sugar and cinnamon. Serves 6.

FRESH FRUIT CRISP

 ½ cup quick-cooking rolled oats
 ½ cup packed brown sugar
 ¼ cup all-purpose flour
 ½ teaspoon ground cinnamon
 ¼ cup butter or margarine
 2 pounds apples (6 medium) or 2½ pounds peaches (10 medium)
 2 tablespoons granulated sugar
 Vanilla ice cream   Oven 350°

Combine oats, brown sugar, flour, cinnamon, and dash *salt*. Cut in butter till mixture resembles coarse crumbs; set aside. Peel, core, and slice fruit to make 5 to 6 cups. Place fruit in a 10×6×2-inch baking dish. Sprinkle with granulated sugar. Sprinkle crumb mixture over all. Bake in a 350° oven for 40 to 45 minutes. Serve with ice cream. Serves 6.

CHOCOLATE POTS DE CRÈME

  1 cup light cream
  1 4-ounce package German sweet chocolate, coarsely chopped
  1 tablespoon sugar
    Dash salt
  3 beaten egg yolks
  ½ teaspoon vanilla
    Whipped cream (optional)

In a heavy small saucepan combine light cream, chopped chocolate, sugar, and salt. Cook and stir over medium-low heat till smooth and *slightly thickened*. Gradually stir about *half* of the hot mixture into beaten egg yolks; return all to saucepan. Cook and stir over medium-low heat 2 to 3 minutes more. Remove from heat; stir in vanilla. Pour into 4 to 6 pots de crème cups or individual small sherbet dishes. Cover and chill several hours or overnight till firm. Garnish with whipped cream, if desired. Makes 4 to 6 servings.

SOUR CREAM CHEESECAKE

  1¾ cups fine graham cracker crumbs
   ¼ cup finely chopped walnuts
   ½ teaspoon ground cinnamon
   ½ cup butter or margarine, melted
    2 8-ounce packages cream cheese, softened
    1 cup sugar
    2 teaspoons vanilla
   ¼ teaspoon almond extract
    3 eggs
    3 cups dairy sour cream   Oven 375°

Combine crumbs, nuts, and cinnamon; add butter or

margarine, stirring till well combined. Reserve ¼ cup for top; press remainder onto bottom and 2½ inches up sides of an 8-inch springform pan or 2 inches up sides of a 9-inch springform pan. In a large mixer bowl beat together cream cheese, sugar, vanilla, almond extract, and ¼ teaspoon *salt* just till smooth. *Do not overbeat.* Add eggs, beating at low speed of electric mixer just till combined. Stir in sour cream. Turn into prepared crust. Sprinkle reserved crumbs atop. Bake in a 375° oven for 50 to 55 minutes or till a knife inserted near center comes out almost clean. Cool on a wire rack; chill 4 to 5 hours. Makes 12 servings.

LEMON PUDDING CAKE

- ¾ cup sugar
- ¼ cup all-purpose flour
- Dash salt
- 3 tablespoons butter, melted
- 1½ teaspoons finely shredded lemon peel
- ¼ cup lemon juice
- 3 beaten egg yolks
- 1½ cups milk
- 3 egg whites   Oven 350°

In a large mixing bowl combine sugar, flour, and salt. Stir in melted butter, lemon peel, and lemon juice. In a small bowl combine egg yolks and milk; add to flour mixture. In a mixer bowl beat egg whites to stiff peaks. Gently fold egg whites into lemon batter. Turn into an ungreased 8×8×2-inch baking pan. Place in a larger pan on oven rack. Pour hot water into larger pan to a depth of 1 inch. Bake in a 350° oven for 35 to 40 minutes or till top is golden and springs back when touched. Serve warm or chilled in individual dessert dishes. Makes 6 to 8 servings.

BAKED APPLES

- 6 large baking apples
- ¾ cup raisins or snipped pitted dates
- ½ cup packed brown sugar
- ½ cup water
- 1 tablespoon butter or margarine
- ½ teaspoon ground cinnamon
- ½ teaspoon ground nutmeg
  Light cream or vanilla ice cream   Oven 350°

Core apples; peel off a strip around top of each. Place apples in a 10×6×2-inch baking dish. Fill apples with raisins or dates. In a saucepan combine brown sugar, water, butter or margarine, cinnamon, and nutmeg; bring to boiling. Pour hot sugar mixture around apples. Bake, uncovered, in a 350° oven about 1 hour or till apples are tender, basting occasionally with the sugar mixture. Serve warm with light cream or ice cream. Makes 6 servings.

CRÊPES SUZETTE

- ½ cup butter or margarine
- ½ cup orange liqueur
- ½ cup orange juice
- 6 tablespoons sugar
  Basic Dessert Crêpes
- ¼ cup brandy

For sauce, in a skillet or chafing dish combine butter, liqueur, orange juice, and sugar; cook and stir till bubbly.

To assemble, fold a Basic Dessert Crêpe in half, browned side out; fold in half again, forming a triangle. Repeat with remaining crêpes. Arrange crêpes in sauce. Simmer till sauce thickens slightly, spooning sauce over crêpes as they heat. In a small saucepan heat the brandy over low heat just till hot. Ignite and pour flaming brandy over crêpes. Serves 8.

Basic Dessert Crêpes: Combine 1½ cups *milk*, 1 cup *all-purpose flour*, 2 *eggs*, 2 tablespoons *sugar*, 1 tablespoon *cooking oil*, and ⅛ teaspoon *salt*. Beat with a rotary beater till combined. Heat a lightly greased 6-inch skillet. Remove from heat. Spoon in 2 tablespoons batter; lift and tilt skillet to spread batter. Return to heat; brown on one side. (*Or*, cook on an inverted crêpe pan.) Invert pan over paper toweling; remove crêpe. Repeat to make 16 to 18 crêpes, greasing skillet occasionally.

MERINGUE SHELLS

Oven 275°

Let 3 *egg whites* stand in a small mixer bowl about 1 hour or till they come to room temperature. Meanwhile, cover baking sheets with brown paper. Draw eight 3-inch circles or one 9-inch circle; set aside. Add 1 teaspoon *vanilla*, ¼ teaspoon *cream of tartar*, and dash *salt* to egg whites. Beat to soft peaks. Gradually add 1 cup *sugar*, beating till very stiff peaks form. Spread meringue over circles on paper to make 8 individual shells or one 9-inch meringue shell; use the back of a spoon to shape into shells. Bake either size in a 275° oven for 1 hour. Turn off oven and let dry in oven, with door closed, for at least 1 hour. Peel off paper. To serve, fill shells with ice cream or pudding and top with fruit or ice cream topping. If necessary to store shells before serving, place in a plastic bag or airtight container. Makes 8 servings.

BAKED ALASKA

Use different flavors of ice cream and cake—
- 2 pints or 1 quart brick-style ice cream*
- 1 1-inch-thick piece sponge cake or layer cake
- 5 egg whites
- 1 teaspoon vanilla
- ½ teaspoon cream of tartar
- ⅔ cup sugar

Oven 500°

Lay ice cream bricks side by side; measure length and width. Trim cake 1 inch larger on all sides than ice cream measurements. Place cake on a piece of foil. Center ice cream on cake. Cover; freeze till firm. At serving time, beat together egg whites, vanilla, and cream of tartar to soft peaks. Gradually add sugar, beating to stiff peaks. Transfer cake with ice cream to a baking sheet. Spread with egg white mixture, sealing to edges of cake and baking sheet all around. Swirl to make peaks. Place oven rack in lowest position. Bake in a 500° oven about 3 minutes or till golden. Slice; serve immediately. Serves 8.

*Note: If you can't locate brick-style ice cream, reshape the ice cream you have to fit atop a round cake base. Select a mixing bowl with a diameter 2 inches smaller than the diameter of a 1-inch-thick round layer cake. Stir ice cream in mixing bowl just enough to soften. Cover; freeze till firm. Center ice cream on cake; continue as directed.

EGGS & CHEESE

EGGS BENEDICT

- 6 slices Canadian-style bacon
- 6 eggs
  Classic Hollandaise Sauce (see recipe, page 157)
- 6 rusks or 3 English muffins, split, toasted, and buttered

In a 12-inch skillet lightly brown bacon over medium heat for 3 minutes on each side. Cover; keep warm. Lightly grease a 10-inch skillet. Add water to half-fill the skillet; bring to boiling. Reduce heat to maintain a simmer. Break 1 egg into a small dish. Carefully slide egg into water, holding lip of dish as close to water as possible. Repeat with remaining eggs so that each has an equal amount of space. Simmer, uncovered, 3 to 5 minutes or till eggs are just soft-cooked. Remove with a slotted spoon; place eggs in a large pan of warm water to keep warm while preparing Classic Hollandaise Sauce. To serve, top each rusk or English muffin half with a bacon slice and an egg; spoon on sauce. Garnish with parsley or sprinkle lightly with paprika, if desired. Makes 6 servings.

DENVER SCRAMBLE

- 1 cup diced fully cooked ham
- 1 2-ounce can mushroom stems and pieces, drained
- ¼ cup chopped onion
- 2 tablespoons chopped green pepper
- 2 tablespoons butter or margarine
- 8 eggs
- ⅓ cup milk

In a 10-inch skillet cook ham, mushrooms, onion, and green pepper in butter or margarine over medium heat about 5 minutes or till vegetables are tender but not brown. Beat together eggs, milk, ¼ teaspoon *salt*, and dash *pepper*; add to skillet. Cook, without stirring, till mixture begins to set on the bottom and around edges. Using a large spoon or spatula, lift and fold partially cooked egg mixture so uncooked portion flows underneath. Continue cooking over medium heat about 4 minutes or till eggs are cooked throughout but are still glossy and moist. Serve immediately. Serves 4.

FARMER'S BREAKFAST

- ¼ cup chopped onion
- ¼ cup butter or margarine
- 2 medium potatoes, peeled and finely chopped (2 cups)
- 1 teaspoon water
- 6 eggs
- 2 tablespoons milk
- 1 cup diced fully cooked ham

In a 10-inch skillet cook onion in butter or margarine till tender. Add potatoes, water, and ¼ teaspoon *salt*.

Cover and cook over medium heat about 10 minutes or till potatoes are tender, stirring occasionally. Beat together eggs, milk, ¼ teaspoon *salt*, and dash *pepper*; stir in ham. Pour over potato mixture. Cook, without stirring, till mixture begins to set on the bottom and around edges. Using a large spoon or spatula, lift and fold partially cooked egg mixture so uncooked portion flows underneath. Continue cooking over medium heat about 4 minutes or till eggs are cooked throughout but still glossy and moist. Serve immediately. Makes 4 servings.

EGG-SAUSAGE CASSEROLE

- 1 pound bulk pork sausage
- ¼ cup butter or margarine
- ¼ cup all-purpose flour
- ½ teaspoon salt
- 2 cups milk
- 4 hard-cooked eggs, sliced
- 1 17-ounce can whole kernel corn, drained
- ¾ cup soft bread crumbs (1 slice)
- 1 tablespoon butter or margarine, melted

Oven 350°

In a skillet cook sausage till browned; drain off fat. In a saucepan melt the ¼ cup butter or margarine; stir in flour and salt. Add milk all at once. Cook and stir till mixture is thickened and bubbly. Cook and stir 1 to 2 minutes more. Stir in cooked sausage, sliced eggs, and drained corn. Pour mixture into a 1½-quart casserole. Toss bread crumbs with melted butter or margarine; sprinkle atop casserole. Bake, uncovered, in a 350° oven for 30 minutes or till heated through. Makes 6 servings.

EASY CHEESE EGGS A LA KING

- ¼ cup chopped celery
- ¼ cup chopped green pepper
- ¼ cup finely chopped onion
- 2 tablespoons butter or margarine
- 1 10¾-ounce can condensed cream of celery soup
- 1 cup shredded American cheese (4 ounces)
- ½ cup milk
- 4 hard-cooked eggs, sliced
- 2 tablespoons chopped pimiento
- 4 slices bread, toasted and buttered

In a saucepan cover and cook celery, green pepper, and onion in butter or margarine till tender but not brown. Stir in celery soup, cheese, and milk; heat and stir till cheese melts. Gently stir in sliced eggs and pimiento. Serve spooned over buttered toast. Makes 4 servings.

EGGS FLORENTINE

- 1 10-ounce package frozen chopped spinach, cooked and drained
- 1 11-ounce can condensed cheddar cheese soup
- 4 eggs
- 2 tablespoons milk
- 1 teaspoon minced dried onion
- 1 teaspoon prepared mustard
- ½ cup croutons

Combine spinach and *half* of the cheese soup. Spoon into four 8-ounce individual casseroles; spread evenly on bottom and halfway up sides of casseroles. Break 1 egg into *each* dish. Bake in a 350° oven 20 to 25 minutes or till eggs are firm. In a saucepan heat together remaining soup, the milk, onion, and mustard. Spoon over eggs. Sprinkle *each* with some of the croutons. Makes 4 servings.

FRENCH OMELET

- 2 eggs
- 1 tablespoon water
- ⅛ teaspoon salt
- Dash pepper
- 1 tablespoon butter or margarine

Beat together the eggs, water, salt, and pepper with a fork till combined but not frothy. In a 6- or 8-inch skillet with flared sides, heat the butter till it sizzles and browns slightly. Lift and tilt the pan to coat the sides. Add egg mixture; cook over medium heat. As eggs set, run a spatula around edge of the skillet, lifting the eggs to allow the uncooked portion to flow underneath. When eggs are set but still shiny, remove from heat. Fold omelet in half. (If making a filled omelet, spoon the filling across center. Fold ⅓ of omelet over filling. Overlap remaining ⅓ atop filling.) Slide omelet to edge of pan. Tilt skillet, then invert to roll omelet out onto a warm serving plate. Makes 1 serving.

Mushroom French Omelet: Prepare French Omelet as above, *except* cook ⅓ cup sliced fresh *mushrooms* in 1 tablespoon *butter or margarine*; use to fill omelet. Continue as directed.

Cheese French Omelet: Prepare French Omelet as above, *except* sprinkle ¼ cup cheddar, Swiss, Monterey Jack, mozzarella, or American *cheese* in center of omelet. Continue as directed. If desired, top omelet with additional shredded cheese and snipped parsley.

Vegetable French Omelet: Prepare French Omelet as on previous page *except* cook ⅓ cup sliced *green onion, asparagus, zucchini, celery, green pepper, or bean sprouts* in 1 tablespoon *butter or margarine*. Use to fill omelet. Continue as directed. Top with 1 tablespoon grated *Parmesan cheese*.

DEVILED EGGS

   6 **hard-cooked eggs**
   ¼ **cup mayonnaise or salad dressing**
   1 **teaspoon vinegar**
   1 **teaspoon prepared mustard**

Halve hard-cooked eggs lengthwise; remove yolks and mash with a fork. Stir in mayonnaise, vinegar, mustard, and ⅛ teaspoon *salt*. Stuff egg whites with yolk mixture. Garnish with paprika or parsley, if desired. Makes 12 servings.

Italian-Style Deviled Eggs: Prepare Deviled Eggs as above, *except* omit mayonnaise, vinegar, and mustard. Add 3 tablespoons *creamy Italian salad dressing* to mashed yolks. Stuff egg whites with yolk mixture.

CLASSIC QUICHE LORRAINE

Oven 450°

Cook 8 slices *bacon* till crisp; drain, reserving 2 tablespoons drippings. Crumble bacon; set aside. Cook 1 medium *onion*, thinly sliced, in reserved drippings till tender; drain. Stir together 4 beaten *eggs*, 1 cup *light cream*, 1 cup *milk*, 1 tablespoon *all-purpose flour*, ½ teaspoon *salt*, and dash ground *nutmeg*. Stir in the bacon, onion, and 1½ cups shredded *Swiss cheese*; mix well.

Prepare *Pastry for Single-Crust Pie* (see recipe, page 110). To keep crust in shape, line the unpricked pastry shell with a double thickness of heavy-duty foil. Bake in a 450° oven for 5 minutes. Remove foil. Bake 5 to 7 minutes more or till pastry is nearly done. Remove from oven; reduce oven temperature to 325°. Pour cheese mixture into *hot* pastry shell. If necessary, cover edge of crust with foil to prevent overbrowning. Bake in a 325° oven for 45 to 50 minutes or till a knife inserted near center comes out clean. Let stand 10 minutes before serving. Makes 6 servings.

BAKED EGGS

Baked eggs are also called shirred eggs. If desired, they may be baked in ramekins, which are individual baking dishes—

Butter or margarine
6 eggs
2 tablespoons light cream or milk
6 tablespoons shredded American cheese (optional)   Oven 325°

Butter a custard cup for *each* egg. Carefully break eggs into the prepared custard cups; sprinkle with salt and pepper. Add *1 teaspoon* of the light cream or milk to *each* egg-filled cup. Set cups in a baking pan; place on oven rack. Pour hot water around cups in pan to a depth of 1 inch. Bake in a 325° oven about 20 minutes or till eggs are firm.

If desired, after 15 minutes of baking, top *each* egg with *1 tablespoon* of the shredded American cheese. Continue baking for 5 to 10 minutes more or till eggs are cooked and cheese is melted. Makes 3 servings.

OMELET SANDWICH PUFF

Oven 350°

Cook 4 slices *bacon* till crisp. Remove bacon; crumble and set aside. Beat together 2 *egg yolks*, 1 whole *egg*, 1 tablespoon *milk*, and ⅛ teaspoon *onion salt*. Add crumbled bacon. In a small skillet melt 2 teaspoons *butter*. Pour in egg mixture; cook over medium heat. As eggs set, run a spatula around edge of skillet, lifting the eggs to allow uncooked portion to flow underneath. When eggs are set but still shiny, fold in half; cut into 2 pieces crosswise.

On a baking sheet place *each* half of the egg mixture on 1 slice of toasted and buttered *bread*. Top *each* with 1 *cheese slice*. Beat 2 *egg whites* till stiff peaks form. Spread the beaten egg whites over both sandwiches. Sprinkle with salt and pepper. Bake in a 350° oven about 10 minutes or till golden. Serve immediately. Makes 2 sandwiches.

WELSH RABBIT

- 1½ cups shredded cheddar or American cheese (6 ounces)
- ¾ cup milk
- 1 teaspoon dry mustard
- 1 teaspoon Worcestershire sauce
- Dash cayenne
- 1 beaten egg
- 4 slices bread, toasted, or poached eggs

For cheese sauce, in a heavy saucepan combine shredded cheese, milk, mustard, Worcestershire sauce, and cayenne. Cook over low heat, stirring constantly, till cheese melts. Slowly stir about *half* of the hot cheese mixture into 1 beaten *egg*; return all to remaining mixture in pan. Cook and stir over low heat till mixture thickens and just bubbles. Serve at once over toast or poached eggs. Makes 4 servings.

Beer Rabbit: Prepare Welsh Rabbit as above, *except* substitute *beer* for the milk. Top each serving with 2 slices of crisp-cooked *bacon*, halved crosswise.

CLASSIC CHEESE FONDUE

- 6 cups coarsely shredded Gruyère or Swiss cheese (24 ounces)
- ¼ cup all-purpose flour
- 1 clove garlic, halved
- 2½ cups dry white wine
- 2 tablespoons kirsch or dry sherry
- Dash pepper
- Dash ground nutmeg
- French or Italian bread, cubed

Toss together cheese and flour; set aside. Rub bottom and sides of fondue pot with garlic cloves; discard garlic. Set fondue pot aside. In a large saucepan heat wine over low heat till small bubbles rise to surface. Just before wine boils, stir in cheese, little by little, making sure cheese has melted before adding more. (Stir *constantly* and continue to add cheese till all is mixed in.) Stir till fondue bubbles gently. Stir in kirsch or dry sherry, pepper, and nutmeg. Pour into a fondue pot; keep fondue bubbling gently over fondue burner. Serve with bread cubes (spear bread cubes with a fondue fork). Serves 10.

CLASSIC CHEESE STRATA

  8 slices day-old bread
  8 ounces American or Swiss cheese, sliced
  4 eggs
2½ cups milk
 ¼ cup finely chopped onion
 ½ teaspoon prepared mustard
    Paprika   Oven 325°

Trim crusts from 4 slices of the bread. Cut trimmed slices in half diagonally to make 8 triangles; set aside. Arrange trimmings and remaining 4 slices of untrimmed bread to cover bottom of a 9×9×2-inch baking pan. Place cheese slices over bread in pan. Arrange the reserved 8 bread triangles in 2 rows over cheese. (Points will slightly overlap bases of preceding triangles.) Beat eggs; stir in milk, chopped onion, mustard, 1½ teaspoons *salt*, and dash *pepper*. Pour over bread and cheese layers. Sprinkle with paprika. Cover; let chill in refrigerator several hours or overnight. Bake, uncovered, in a 325° oven 1¼ hours or till a knife inserted near center comes out clean. Let stand 5 minutes before serving. Serves 6.

FISH & SEAFOOD

Add variety to your menus by including fish dishes often. Fish has a delicate flavor and tender texture. It's versatile and also cooks quickly. Cooking fish to the right doneness is important. Use the test below.

Insert fork tines into the fish at a 45-degree angle. Twist the fork gently. If fish resists flaking and is still translucent, it's not done. If it flakes apart easily and is milky white, it's done. A dry and mealy texture indicates overcooked fish.

FISH FLORENTINE

- 6 frozen breaded fish portions
- 1 10-ounce package frozen chopped spinach
- 1 11-ounce can condensed cheddar cheese soup
- 1 8-ounce can water chestnuts, drained and coarsely chopped
- 3 tablespoons bacon bits   Oven 350°

Prepare fish following package directions. Cook spinach following package directions; drain well. In a saucepan stir soup, water chestnuts, and bacon bits into spinach; heat through. Turn into a 10×6×2-inch baking dish or 1½-quart casserole. Top with fish. Bake in a 350° oven for 10 minutes or till hot. Serve with halved lemon slices, if desired. Serves 6.

Thawing Fish

Place the frozen wrapped package in the refrigerator. A 16-ounce package takes about 24 hours to thaw. For faster thawing (1 to 2 hours per 1-pound package), set the wrapped package under cold running water. *Do not thaw the fish at room temperature or in warm water; do not refreeze fish. Also, do not thaw breaded fish portions.*

STACKED SOLE

- 2 pounds fresh or frozen sole fillets or other fish fillets
- 2 cups sliced fresh mushrooms
- 3 tablespoons sliced green onion
- 1 clove garlic, minced
- 2 tablespoons butter or margarine
- 1 6½-ounce can minced clams, drained
- 2 tablespoons snipped parsley
- 1 tablespoon lemon juice
- ¾ teaspoon dried oregano, crushed
- ¼ teaspoon salt
  Shrimp Sauce   Oven 350°

Thaw fish, if frozen. In a skillet cook mushrooms, onion, and garlic in butter till tender but not brown. Remove from heat. Stir in drained clams, parsley, lemon juice, the oregano, salt, and ⅛ teaspoon *pepper*. In a 13×9×2-inch baking dish lay *half* of the fish fillets in a single layer. Spoon mushroom mixture over each fillet. Stack remaining fillets over top. Bake, covered, in a 350° oven for 25 minutes. Uncover; bake

10 to 15 minutes more or till fish flakes easily when tested with a fork. With a slotted spatula, transfer fish stacks to a serving platter. Spoon Shrimp Sauce over. Garnish with cherry tomatoes and endive or parsley, if desired. Serves 6 to 8.

Shrimp Sauce: In a saucepan melt 2 tablespoons *butter or margarine*. Stir in 1 tablespoon *lemon juice* and, if desired, 2 tablespoons snipped *parsley*. Drain one 4½-ounce can *tiny shrimp*; stir shrimp into butter mixture. Heat sauce through.

BAKED FISH WITH MUSHROOMS

    4 fresh or frozen fish fillets or steaks
    2 slices bacon
    1 cup sliced fresh mushrooms or one
        6-ounce can sliced mushrooms,
        drained
    ½ cup green onion bias-sliced into 1-inch
        lengths
    3 tablespoons butter or margarine
    ¼ teaspoon dried tarragon, crushed
      Paprika   Oven 350°

Thaw fish, if frozen. In a skillet cook bacon; reserve drippings. Crumble bacon; set aside. Cook mushrooms and onion in drippings till tender. Place fish in a 12×7½×2-inch baking dish; sprinkle with salt. Combine mushrooms, onion, butter, and tarragon. Spread atop fish; sprinkle with paprika. Bake in a 350° oven 15 to 20 minutes or till fish flakes easily when tested with a fork. (Thin fillets will bake in less time.) Garnish with the crumbled bacon. Makes 4 servings.

OVEN-FRIED FISH

  1 pound fresh or frozen fish fillets or steaks
     or three 10- to 12-ounce fresh or
     frozen pan-dressed trout or other fish
  1 beaten egg
½ cup fine dry bread crumbs
¼ cup butter or margarine, melted
  1 tablespoon lemon juice   Oven 500°

Thaw fish, if frozen. If using a fillet block, cut block into 3 portions. Dip fish into beaten egg, then into bread crumbs. Place coated fish in a well-greased, shallow baking pan. Sprinkle with salt and pepper. Drizzle a mixture of melted butter or margarine and lemon juice over fish. Bake in a 500° oven until golden and fish flakes easily when tested with a fork. Allow 5 to 6 minutes for each ½ inch of thickness. Serves 3.

QUICK FISH-POTATO SUPPER

   1 12-ounce package frozen loose-pack
      hashed brown potatoes, thawed
   4 beaten eggs
   2 cups milk
   1 tablespoon minced dried onion
1¼ teaspoons seasoned salt
   1 teaspoon dried dillweed
⅛ teaspoon pepper
   1 cup shredded American cheese
   1 14-ounce package frozen fish
     sticks   Oven 350°

Break up potatoes; set aside. In a bowl combine eggs, milk, onion, seasoned salt, dillweed, and pepper. Stir in potatoes and cheese. Turn into a 12×7½×2-inch baking dish. Arrange fish sticks atop. Bake in a 350° oven for 55 to 60 minutes or till center is nearly set. Let stand 10 minutes before serving. Serves 6.

BAKED FISH A L'ORANGE

- 2 pounds fresh or frozen halibut steaks or other fish steaks
- ½ cup finely chopped onion
- 2 cloves garlic, minced
- 2 tablespoons cooking oil
- 2 tablespoons snipped parsley
- ½ cup orange juice
- 1 tablespoon lemon juice   Oven 400°

Thaw fish, if frozen. Arrange in a 12×7½×2-inch baking dish. Cook onion and garlic in oil till onion is tender but not brown. Stir in parsley, 1 teaspoon *salt*, and ⅛ teaspoon *pepper*. Spread mixture over fish. Combine orange and lemon juices; pour evenly over all. Bake, covered, in a 400° oven for 20 to 25 minutes or till fish flakes easily with a fork. If desired, arrange hard-cooked egg wedges atop fish, sprinkle with paprika, and garnish with orange slices. Makes 6 servings.

BAKED FILLETS AND STEAKS   Oven 450°

Use 2 pounds fresh *or* frozen *fish fillets or steaks*. Thaw fish, if frozen. Cut fillets into 6 portions. Place fish in a greased baking pan in a single layer with skin side down. Tuck under thin edges. Brush tops with 3 tablespoons melted *butter*. Season. Bake, uncovered, in a 450° oven until fish flakes easily when tested with a fork. Allow 5 to 6 minutes for each ½ inch of thickness. Makes 6 servings.

COMPANY CREAMED TUNA

    2 tablespoons finely chopped onion
    3 tablespoons butter or margarine
    3 tablespoons all-purpose flour
1¼ cups milk
    ½ cup dairy sour cream
    1 6½-ounce can tuna, drained
    3 tablespoons dry white wine
    2 tablespoons snipped parsley
    4 baked patty shells or buttered toast points

In a saucepan cook onion in butter till tender. Stir in flour, ¼ teaspoon *salt*, and dash *pepper*. Add milk all at once; cook quickly, stirring constantly, until mixture thickens and bubbles. Stir about *1 cup* of the hot milk mixture into sour cream; return all to saucepan. Add tuna, wine, and parsley. Heat through. Serve in patty shells or spoon over hot buttered toast points. Sprinkle with toasted almonds, if desired. Makes 4 servings.

BAKED TUNA PATTIES

    ¼ cup finely chopped celery
    6 tablespoons butter or margarine
    3 tablespoons all-purpose flour
    ¼ teaspoon paprika
    ¾ cup milk
    1 9¼-ounce can tuna, drained
    2 cups soft bread crumbs
    2 tablespoons chopped green onion
    1 egg
    ⅔ cup finely crushed round cheese
       crackers (about 20)   Oven 350°

For sauce, in a saucepan cook celery in *3 tablespoons* of the butter till tender. Stir in flour, paprika, and ¼ teaspoon *salt*. Stir in milk. Cook and stir till thickened and bubbly. Cool slightly. Flake tuna. Mix into sauce with bread crumbs and onion. Form into eight 2½-inch patties. Beat together egg and 1 tablespoon *water*. Dip patties into egg mixture, then into crackers. Place in a lightly greased 11×7×1½-inch baking pan. Melt remaining butter. Drizzle over patties. Bake in a 350° oven for 20 to 25 minutes or till golden. Makes 4 servings.

SALMON LOAF

- 1 16-ounce can salmon, drained
- 2 cups soft bread crumbs (about 2½ slices)
- 2 tablespoons chopped green onion
- 1 tablespoon butter or margarine, melted
- ½ teaspoon salt
- ⅛ teaspoon pepper
- ½ cup milk
- 1 slightly beaten egg   Oven 350°

Flake salmon, discarding skin and bones. In a bowl combine salmon, bread crumbs, chopped onion, butter or margarine, salt, and pepper. Mix well. Combine milk and egg; add to salmon mixture and mix thoroughly. Shape into a loaf in a greased shallow baking pan or in a greased 7½×3½×2-inch loaf pan. Bake in a 350° oven for 35 to 40 minutes. If desired, serve with Cheese Sauce (see recipe, page 156). Makes 3 or 4 servings.

SKILLET DILLED SALMON PATTIES

- 1 16-ounce can salmon
- ½ cup chopped onion
- 2 tablespoons butter or margarine
- ⅔ cup fine dry bread crumbs
- 2 beaten eggs
- 1 teaspoon dried dillweed
- ½ teaspoon dry mustard
- 2 tablespoons shortening or cooking oil

Drain salmon, reserving ⅓ cup liquid. Discard bones and skin from salmon; flake meat. Cook onion in butter or margarine till tender but not brown. Remove from heat. Add reserved salmon liquid, ⅓ *cup* of the bread crumbs, beaten eggs, dillweed, mustard, and flaked salmon; mix well. Shape into 4 patties; coat with remaining crumbs.

In a skillet melt shortening or heat oil. Cook patties over medium heat about 3 minutes or till browned. Carefully turn; brown other side about 3 minutes more. If desired, spoon Lemon-Chive Sauce (see recipe, page 157) over patties or serve with lemon wedges or creamed peas. Makes 4 servings.

BOILED SHELLFISH

A basic way to prepare shellfish, especially when the meat will be used in other recipes—

Shrimp: Heat 6 cups *water* and 2 tablespoons *salt* to boiling. Add 2 pounds fresh or frozen *shelled or unshelled shrimp;* simmer 1 to 3 minutes or till shrimp turn pink. Drain. Makes 6 to 8 servings.

Scallops: Heat 4 cups *water* and 2 teaspoons *salt* to boiling. Add 2 pounds fresh or thawed frozen *scallops*. Simmer for 1 minute or till scallops are opaque. Drain. Serves 8.

Lobster Tails: Heat to boiling enough *salted water* to cover 2 pounds frozen *lobster tails*. Simmer the 3-ounce tails for 3 to 4 minutes; the 6-ounce tails for 8 minutes; or the 8-ounce tails for 11 minutes. Drain. Makes about 4 servings.

Crabs: Heat to boiling enough *salted water* to cover 2 pounds *crabs*. Plunge live, scrubbed Dungeness or hard-shell blue crabs into boiling water. Simmer Dungeness crabs 8 minutes per pound; simmer blue crabs for 15 minutes. Drain. Makes about 2 servings.

BROILED SHRIMP

- 2 **pounds fresh or frozen large shrimp in shells**
- ¼ **cup butter or margarine, melted**
- 2 **tablespoons lemon juice**
- **Dash bottled hot pepper sauce**

Thaw shrimp, if frozen. Remove shells and devein. Combine butter, lemon juice, and hot pepper sauce. Brush some mixture over shrimp.

To broil in the oven, place shrimp on a well-greased broiler rack and broil 4 to 5 inches from heat for 4 minutes. Turn and brush with butter mixture. Broil 2 to 4 minutes more or till shrimp are done. To cook on an outdoor grill, thread shrimp on skewers and grill over *hot* coals for 4 minutes. Turn and brush with butter mixture. Grill 4 to 5 minutes more or till shrimp are done. Season shrimp lightly with salt. Makes 6 servings.

LOBSTER NEWBURG

- ¼ cup butter or margarine
- 2 tablespoons all-purpose flour
- 1½ cups light cream
- 3 beaten egg yolks
- 2 5-ounce cans lobster, drained, broken into large pieces, and cartilage removed, *or* 10 ounces cooked lobster
- 3 tablespoons dry white wine
- 2 teaspoons lemon juice
- ¼ teaspoon salt
- Paprika
- 4 baked patty shells

Melt butter or margarine in a saucepan; stir in flour. Add cream all at once. Cook and stir till thickened and bubbly. Stir about *half* of the hot mixture into egg yolks; return to hot mixture. Cook and stir till thickened but *do not boil*. Add lobster; heat through. Stir in wine, lemon juice, and salt. Sprinkle with a little paprika. Spoon into patty shells. Garnish with fresh parsley sprigs, if desired. Serves 4.

Crab Newburg: Prepare Lobster Newburg as above, *except* substitute two 7-ounce cans *crab meat*, drained, flaked, and cartilage removed, *or* two 6-ounce packages frozen *crab meat*, thawed, for the lobster. Continue as directed.

Shrimp Newburg: Prepare Lobster Newburg as above, *except* substitute 1½ cups cooked shelled *shrimp or* two 4½-ounce cans *shrimp*, drained, for the lobster. Continue.

MEAT

TERIYAKI ROAST BEEF

   1 6- to 7-pound boneless beef rib roast
   1 cup soy sauce
  ½ cup cooking oil
  ¼ cup light molasses
   1 tablespoon ground ginger
   1 tablespoon dry mustard
   4 cloves garlic, minced   Oven 325°

Place meat in a plastic bag; set in a deep bowl. For marinade, combine remaining ingredients; pour over meat. Close bag. Chill overnight, turning occasionally.

Remove meat, reserving marinade. Place meat, fat side up, on a rack in a shallow roasting pan. Sprinkle with a little salt and pepper. Insert a meat thermometer. Roast in a 325° oven for 3 to 3¾ hours for rare or till thermometer registers 140°; 3½ to 4¼ hours for medium (160°); or 4 to 4¾ hours for well-done (170°). During roasting, baste several times with the reserved marinade.

Remove roast from oven; cover with foil. Let stand about 15 minutes. Remove strings and carve thinly across the grain. Serves 14.

SAVORY STUFFED RIB ROAST

- 6 slices bacon
- ¼ cup chopped onion
- 1 clove garlic, minced
- 3 tablespoons chopped pimiento-stuffed olives
- 1 4- to 5-pound boneless beef rib roast   Oven 325°

Crisp-cook and crumble bacon; drain, reserving 1 tablespoon of the drippings. Set bacon aside. Cook onion and garlic in reserved drippings till tender. Remove from heat. Stir in olives and bacon. Unroll roast; spread bacon mixture over meat. Reroll roast; tie securely.

Place meat, fat side up, on a rack in a shallow roasting pan. Sprinkle with a little salt and pepper. Insert a meat thermometer. Roast in a 325° oven 2½ to 3 hours for rare or till thermometer registers 140°. Let roast stand covered with foil about 15 minutes. Remove strings and carve. Serve 8 to 10.

ROAST WITH BARBECUE GRAVY

- 1 4-pound beef chuck pot roast
- 2 tablespoons cooking oil
- ¾ cup bottled barbecue sauce
- ¼ cup orange marmalade
- 1 tablespoon vinegar
- 2 tablespoons cornstarch

Trim excess fat from meat. In a Dutch oven brown meat on all sides in hot oil. Sprinkle with salt and pepper. Combine barbecue sauce, marmalade, vinegar, and ½ cup *water*; pour over meat. Cover; simmer about 2¼ hours or till meat is tender. Remove meat to a platter; keep warm. Pour meat juices and fat into a large glass measure. Skim off excess fat. Measure 2 cups liquid (if necessary add water). Return to Dutch oven. Combine cornstarch and 2 tablespoons *cold water*; stir into pan juices. Cook and stir till bubbly. Cook and stir 1 to 2 minutes more. Spoon some gravy over meat; pass remaining gravy. Serves 10.

NEW ENGLAND BOILED DINNER

- **1 3- to 4-pound corned beef brisket**
- **4 medium potatoes, peeled**
- **4 medium carrots**
- **8 small onions**
- **3 medium parsnips, peeled and cut into chunks**
- **2 medium rutabagas, peeled and cut into chunks**
- **1 small cabbage, cored**

Place meat in a Dutch oven; add juices and spices from package, if desired. Add water to cover meat. Bring to boiling; reduce heat and simmer, covered, about 2 hours or till meat is almost tender. Quarter potatoes and carrots; add to pan with onions, parsnips, and rutabagas. Cover; return to boiling. Reduce heat and simmer 15 minutes. Cut cabbage into wedges; add to pan. Cover; cook 15 to 20 minutes more or till meat and vegetables are tender. Transfer meat and vegetables to a platter. Season with salt and pepper. Serves 8.

LONDON BROIL

 1 1- to 1¼-pound beef flank steak
 ⅓ cup cooking oil
 1 teaspoon vinegar
 1 small clove garlic, minced
    Salt
    Freshly ground pepper

Score steak on both sides. Place meat in a plastic bag; set in a deep bowl. Combine oil, vinegar, and garlic; pour over meat. Close bag. Let stand at room temperature 2 to 3 hours, turning several times. Remove meat from marinade; place on an unheated rack in a broiler pan. Broil 3 inches from heat 4 to 5 minutes. Sprinkle with salt and pepper. Turn; broil 4 to 5 minutes more for medium rare. Sprinkle with salt and pepper. Carve into very thin slices diagonally across grain. Serves 4 to 5.

CHICKEN-FRIED ROUND STEAK

 1½ pounds beef round steak, cut ½ inch thick
 1 beaten egg
 1 tablespoon milk
 1 cup finely crushed saltine crackers (28 crackers)
 ¼ cup cooking oil

Pound steak to ¼-inch thickness; cut into 6 pieces. Stir together egg and milk; combine cracker crumbs, ½ teaspoon *salt*, and ¼ teaspoon *pepper*. Dip meat in egg mixture, then in crumbs. In a 12-inch skillet brown meat in hot oil, turning once. Cover; cook over low heat 45 to 60 minutes or till tender. Serves 6.

BROILED SHORT RIBS

- 4 pounds beef short ribs, cut into serving-size pieces
- ⅔ cup catsup
- ¼ cup light molasses
- ¼ cup lemon juice
- 1 tablespoon dry mustard
- ½ teaspoon chili powder
- Dash garlic powder

Trim excess fat from ribs. Sprinkle with some salt and pepper. Place ribs in a Dutch oven; add water to cover. Simmer, covered, about 2 hours or till meat is tender. Drain; place ribs on an unheated rack in a broiler pan. Combine catsup, molasses, lemon juice, mustard, chili powder, and garlic powder; brush some over ribs. Broil 4 to 5 inches from heat for 10 to 15 minutes, turning often and basting with catsup mixture. Serves 6.

DEVILED BEEF ROLLS

- 2 tablespoons regular onion soup mix
- 3 tablespoons horseradish mustard
- 4 beef cubed steaks (1 pound total)
- 1 4-ounce can sliced mushrooms, drained
- 2 tablespoons butter, melted

Mix dry soup mix and 4 teaspoons *water*; let stand 5 minutes. Stir in mustard. Sprinkle steaks with a little pepper. Spread one side of each steak with ¼ of the mustard mixture; top *each* with ¼ of the mushrooms. Roll up steaks and fasten with wooden picks. Brush with butter. Broil 4 to 5 inches from heat 6 minutes. Turn and brush with butter; broil 6 minutes more. Remove picks. Serves 4.

CREAMED DRIED BEEF

In a skillet cook one 3- or 4-ounce package *sliced dried or smoked beef*, snipped, in 2 tablespoons *butter* 3 minutes or till edges curl. Stir 2 tablespoons all-purpose *flour* into butter mixture; add 1⅓ cups *milk* all at once. Cook and stir till thickened and bubbly. Cook and stir 1 to 2 minutes more. Stir in ½ teaspoon *Worcestershire sauce* and dash *pepper*. Spoon over *buttered toast points*. Serves 3 or 4.

SKILLETBURGERS

- 1 pound ground beef
- 1 cup chopped onion
- ½ cup chopped celery
- 1 15-ounce can tomato sauce
- 2 tablespoons quick-cooking rolled oats
- 1 tablespoon brown sugar
- 1 teaspoon Worcestershire sauce
- ½ teaspoon chili powder
  Dash bottled hot pepper sauce
- 14 to 16 hamburger buns, split and toasted

In a skillet cook beef, onion, and celery till beef is browned and onion is tender; drain off excess fat. Stir in tomato sauce, oats, brown sugar, Worcestershire, chili powder, hot pepper sauce, ½ cup *water*, 1 teaspoon *salt*, and ⅛ teaspoon *pepper*. Simmer, uncovered, about 30 minutes or till mixture is of desired consistency. Spoon about ½ *cup* of the meat mixture into *each* bun. Makes 7 or 8 servings.

MUSHROOM STEAK SAUCE

In a medium saucepan cook 2 cups sliced fresh *mushrooms*, ½ cup chopped *onion*, and 1 clove *garlic*, minced, in 3 tablespoons *butter or margarine* about 5 minutes or till tender. Sprinkle with ⅛ teaspoon *salt*, ⅛ teaspoon *pepper*, and ⅛ teaspoon *celery salt*. Spoon over 4 broiled or panbroiled *beef steaks*. Serves 4.

HAMBURGER PIE

  1 pound ground beef
½ cup chopped onion
  1 16-ounce can cut green beans, drained
  1 10¾-ounce can condensed tomato soup
  3 medium potatoes, peeled and quartered (1 pound)
  1 beaten egg
    Milk
½ cup shredded American cheese
    (2 ounces)   Oven 350°

In a large skillet cook ground beef and onion till meat is browned and onion is tender; drain off fat. Stir in beans, soup, ¼ cup *water*, ¾ teaspoon *salt*, and ⅛ teaspoon *pepper*. Turn mixture into a 1½-quart casserole.

In a covered pan cook potatoes in boiling salted water about 20 minutes or just till tender; drain. Mash while hot; stir in egg. Add enough milk to make potatoes fluffy, yet stiff enough to hold their shape. Season with salt and pepper. Drop potatoes in mounds atop meat mixture. Sprinkle with cheese. Bake, uncovered, in a 350° oven for 25 to 30 minutes or till heated through. Makes 4 to 6 servings.

PORCUPINE MEATBALLS

- 1 beaten egg
- 1 10¾-ounce can condensed tomato soup
- ¼ cup long grain rice
- 2 tablespoons finely chopped onion
- 1 tablespoon snipped parsley
- 1 pound ground beef
- 1 teaspoon Worcestershire sauce

In a bowl combine egg and ¼ *cup* of the soup. Stir in uncooked rice, onion, parsley, ½ teaspoon *salt*, and ⅛ teaspoon *pepper*. Add beef and mix well. Shape meat mixture into 20 small balls; place in a 10-inch skillet. Mix remaining soup with Worcestershire and ½ cup *water*; pour over meatballs. Bring to boiling; reduce heat. Cover and simmer 35 to 40 minutes; stir often. Makes 4 to 5 servings.

SHERRIED VEAL POT ROAST

- 1 1½- to 2-pound veal shoulder blade roast
- 2 tablespoons butter or margarine
- 2 small onions, sliced
- 1 bay leaf
- 1 teaspoon instant beef bouillon granules
- ½ teaspoon dried thyme, crushed
- 3 carrots, sliced
- 3 tablespoons all-purpose flour
- ½ cup sliced fresh mushrooms
- 3 tablespoons dry sherry

In a Dutch oven brown meat on all sides in butter. Add *half* of the onions. Add bay leaf, bouillon granules, thyme, 1 cup *water*, 1 teaspoon *salt*, and dash *pepper*. Cover and simmer for 45 minutes. Add remaining onions and the carrots. Simmer, covered, 25 to 30 minutes or till meat and vegetables are tender. Remove meat and vegetables to a platter; keep warm.

Pour meat juices and fat into a glass measure. Skim off excess fat. Measure 1 cup juices (if necessary, add water). Return juices to Dutch oven. Stir ⅓ cup *cold water* into flour; stir into pan juices. Add mushrooms. Cook and stir until thickened and bubbly. Cook and stir 1 to 2 minutes more. Stir in sherry. Season. Serve with veal. Makes 6 servings.

VEAL CORDON BLEU

- 2 slices boiled ham
- 2 slices Swiss cheese
- 1 pound veal leg round steak, cut ¼ inch thick
- ⅔ cup fine dry bread crumbs
- 1 teaspoon snipped parsley
- ⅛ teaspoon pepper
- ¼ cup all-purpose flour
- 1 slightly beaten egg
- ¼ cup butter or margarine

Quarter ham and cheese slices. Cut veal into 4 pieces; pound with a meat mallet to ⅛-inch thickness (each about 8×4 inches). Cut each veal piece in half crosswise. On one half, place 2 quarters *each* of ham and cheese; trim or fold to fit. Cover with second piece of veal; seal edges. Repeat with remaining meats and cheese. Combine bread crumbs, parsley, and pepper. Dip meat in flour, then in beaten egg, then in crumb mixture.

In a skillet melt butter or margarine. Add meat; cook over medium-high heat about 4 minutes per side or till golden brown. Serve at once. Makes 4 servings.

PORK BURGERS

- 1 pound ground pork
- 2 tablespoons chopped green onion
- ¾ teaspoon salt
- ¼ teaspoon ground sage
- ⅛ teaspoon pepper
- 4 hamburger buns, split and toasted

Combine all ingredients except buns. Shape into four ½-inch-thick patties. Place patties on an unheated rack in a broiler pan. Broil patties 3 inches from heat for 8 minutes. Turn; broil 7 minutes more. (*Or*, panbroil patties. Preheat a heavy skillet. Cook patties over medium heat for 6 to 7 minutes per side, or till done. Partially cover skillet to prevent spattering.) Serve on toasted hamburger buns. Serves 4.

BRAISED PORK STEAKS

- 4 pork shoulder blade steaks, cut ½ inch thick (2 to 2½ pounds)
- ½ cup tomato sauce
- ¼ teaspoon ground sage

Trim excess fat from steaks; in a large skillet cook fat trimmings till 2 tablespoons fat accumulate. Discard trimmings. Brown 2 steaks slowly on each side in hot fat; remove steaks. Repeat with remaining 2 steaks. Drain off excess fat. Return all steaks to skillet. Season with salt and pepper. Add tomato sauce and sage. Cover tightly; cook over low heat for 30 to 35 minutes or till meat is tender. Skim excess fat from juices. If necessary, cook down juices to thicken slightly; spoon over meat. Makes 4 servings.

ORANGE-GLAZED RIBS

 4 pounds meaty pork spareribs, cut into serving-size pieces
 ⅔ cup orange marmalade
 3 tablespoons soy sauce
 2 tablespoons lemon juice
 ¾ teaspoon ground ginger
   Orange slices

Oven 450°

Place ribs, meaty side down, in a shallow roasting pan. Roast in a 450° oven for 30 minutes. Remove meat from oven; drain off excess fat. Turn ribs meaty side up. Reduce oven temperature to 350°; continue roasting 30 minutes longer. Meanwhile, prepare glaze. Combine marmalade, soy sauce, lemon juice, and ginger; mix well. Spoon *half* of the mixture over spareribs. Roast 30 minutes more or till tender, spooning remaining glaze over ribs occasionally. Garnish ribs on a serving platter with orange slices. Makes 6 servings.

BASIC BROILED PORK CHOPS AND STEAKS

Set the oven temperature to "broil" and preheat if desired (check instructions for your range). Place meat on an unheated rack in a broiler pan. Broil pork 3 to 4 inches from heat for half the suggested time. Season with salt and pepper. Turn meat using tongs; cook till done. Season again. Follow these times as guideline; pork rib or loin chops cut ¾ to 1 inch thick, 20 to 25 minutes total time; pork shoulder steaks cut ½ to ¾ inch thick, 20 to 22 minutes total time.

CURRIED PORK

- 1 large apple, cored and chopped
- ¼ cup sliced green onion
- 2 teaspoons curry powder
- 1 tablespoon butter or margarine
- 1 10¾-ounce can condensed cream of mushroom soup
- ¾ cup milk
- 2 tablespoons snipped parsley
- 2 cups cubed cooked pork
- 1 cup dairy sour cream
- Hot cooked rice

In a saucepan cook chopped apple, green onion, and curry powder in butter or margarine till onion is tender. Stir in soup, milk, and parsley. Add pork; simmer, uncovered, 10 minutes. Stir in sour cream. Heat through but *do not boil*. Serve over hot cooked rice. Makes 4 servings.

SWEET-SOUR PORK

In a bowl combine 1 beaten *egg*, ¼ cup *cornstarch*, ¼ cup all-purpose *flour*, ¼ cup *chicken broth*, and ½ teaspoon *salt*. Beat till smooth. Use 1 pound boneless pork, cut into 1-inch cubes; dip pork cubes into batter. Fry in deep hot *cooking oil* (365°) for 5 to 6 minutes or till golden. Drain; keep warm.

In a skillet cook 1 large *green pepper*, chopped; ½ cup chopped *carrot*; and 1 clove *garlic*, minced, in 2 tablespoons hot *cooking oil* till vegetables are tender but not brown. Stir in 1¼ cups *chicken broth*, ½ cup *sugar*, ⅓ cup *red wine vinegar*, and 2 teaspoons *soy sauce*. Bring to boiling; boil rapidly 1 minute. Stir ¼ cup *cold water* into 2 tablespoons *cornstarch*. Stir into vegetable mixture. Cook and stir till thickened and bubbly. Cook and stir 1 to 2 minutes more. Stir in pork cubes. Serve with hot cooked rice, if desired. Makes 4 to 6 servings.

HAM CARIBBEAN

- 1 2-pound fully cooked ham center slice, cut 1 inch thick
- 2 oranges
  Orange juice
- 1 tablespoon whole cloves
- ⅓ cup packed brown sugar
- 4 teaspoons cornstarch
- 2 tablespoons rum
- 1 tablespoon honey
- 1 8¼-ounce can pineapple chunks, drained
- ½ cup light raisins   Oven 350°

Slash edge of ham slice; place on a rack in a shallow baking pan. Bake in a 350° oven for 30 minutes. Meanwhile, peel and section oranges over a bowl to catch juice. Set orange sections aside. Measure juice in bowl; add additional orange juice, if necessary, to make ⅓ cup liquid. In a saucepan combine orange juice and whole cloves; bring to boiling. Reduce heat; simmer gently, uncovered, for 5 minutes. Discard cloves. Combine brown sugar and cornstarch; stir in rum and honey. Stir mixture into orange juice. Cook and stir till thickened and bubbly. Cook and stir 1 to 2 minutes more. Stir in orange sections, pineapple chunks, and raisins. Heat through. Spoon over ham. Makes 6 servings.

APRICOT-HAM PATTIES

  2 beaten eggs
  ¾ cup milk
  1½ cups soft bread crumbs (2 slices)
  ½ cup finely snipped dried apricots
  ¼ cup chopped onion
  2 tablespoons snipped parsley
  Dash pepper
  1 pound ground fully cooked ham
  1 pound ground pork
  ⅓ cup packed brown sugar
  1 teaspoon all-purpose flour   Oven 350°

Combine eggs, milk, bread crumbs, dried apricots, onion, parsley, and pepper. Add ground ham and pork; mix well. Shape meat mixture into eight ½-inch-thick patties. Combine brown sugar and flour; sprinkle in bottom of a 15×10×1-inch baking pan. Place patties in pan. Bake in a 350° oven for 40 to 45 minutes. Transfer patties to a serving platter. Stir together the pan juices and spoon over meat. Makes 8 servings.

POTATO-HAM SCALLOP

  2 cups cubed fully cooked ham
  6 medium potatoes, peeled and thinly sliced
     (2 pounds)
  ¼ cup finely chopped onion
  ⅓ cup all-purpose flour
  2 cups milk
  3 tablespoons fine dry bread crumbs
  1 tablespoon butter or margarine, melted
  2 tablespoons finely snipped
     parsley   Oven 350°

Place *half* of the ham in a 2-quart casserole. Cover with *half* of the potatoes and *half* of the onion. Stir *half* of the flour over; season with salt and pepper. Repeat layering ham, potatoes, and onion. Season with additional salt and pepper. Sift remaining flour atop. Pour milk over all. Bake, covered, in a 350° oven for 1 to 1¼ hours or till potatoes are nearly tender. Uncover. Combine bread crumbs and melted butter; sprinkle atop casserole. Top with parsley. Bake 15 minutes more. Serves 4 to 6.

SAUSAGE- AND APPLE-STUFFED SQUASH

- 2 acorn squash, halved
- ¾ pound bulk pork sausage
- ¾ cup chopped celery
- 3 tablespoons chopped onion
- 1 medium cooking apple, peeled, cored, and chopped (1 cup)
- 1 slightly beaten egg
- ½ cup dairy sour cream
- ¾ cup shredded American cheese (3 ounces)

Oven 350°

Place squash halves, cut side down, in a baking pan. Bake in a 350° oven for about 45 minutes or till tender. Sprinkle cut side with salt. In a skillet cook sausage, celery, and onion till meat is browned. Stir in apple; cook 3 minutes more. Drain off fat. Combine egg and sour cream; stir into sausage mixture. Fill squash halves with sausage mixture. Bake 20 minutes. Sprinkle cheese atop. Bake 5 minutes more. Makes 4 servings.

CREAMED BRATWURST

In a 10-inch skillet brown 1½ pounds fully cooked *bratwurst* in 2 tablespoons hot *cooking oil* about 5 minutes; remove from skillet. Slice bratwurst into ½-inch-thick slices; set aside. Add 1 cup chopped *onion*, ½ cup chopped *green pepper*, and 1 teaspoon *dry mustard* to drippings in skillet. Cook and stir till onion is tender but not brown. Stir in 3 tablespoons *all-purpose flour* and ½ teaspoon *salt*. Add 1 cup *chicken broth* and ¾ cup *milk* all at once; cook and stir till thickened and bubbly. Cook and stir 1 to 2 minutes more. Add bratwurst slices. Reduce heat; cover and cook 5 minutes more. Serve with *hot cooked noodles*, if desired. Makes 6 servings.

LAMB CHOPS SUPREME

In a large skillet brown 6 *lamb shoulder chops*, cut ½ inch thick, in 2 tablespoons hot *cooking oil*; sprinkle with salt and pepper. Drain off fat. Add ¾ cup *water*, ¼ cup finely chopped *celery*, ¼ cup sliced *green onion*, 1 teaspoon instant *beef bouillon granules*, and ½ teaspoon dried *thyme*, crushed. Cover; simmer 20 to 25 minutes or till tender. Remove chops to a platter; keep warm. Skim excess fat from drippings. Measure ½ cup drippings; set aside.

For sauce, combine ½ cup *dairy sour cream*, 1 tablespoon *all-purpose flour*, and dash *pepper*. Slowly stir in the reserved drippings. Return mixture to skillet. Add one 2½-ounce jar sliced *mushrooms*, drained, and 2 tablespoons snipped *parsley*. Cook and stir till thickened, just to boiling. Pass sauce with meat. Makes 6 servings.

SAVORY LAMBURGERS

In a mixing bowl combine ¾ cup *soft bread crumbs* (1 slice); one 2-ounce can chopped *mushrooms*, drained; ⅓ cup *milk*; 2 tablespoons finely chopped *onion*; 2 tablespoons chopped *pimiento-stuffed olives*; 1 tablespoon snipped *parsley*; ¼ teaspoon *salt*; and dash *pepper*. Add 1 pound *ground lamb*; mix well. Shape into six ½-inch-thick patties. In a 10-inch skillet cook patties over medium heat for 5 to 7 minutes. Turn; cook 5 to 7 minutes more or till done. (*Or*, place lamb patties on an unheated rack in a broiler pan. Broil 4 to 5 inches from heat for 5 minutes; turn and broil 4 to 5 minutes longer.) Serve on 6 *hamburger buns*, split and toasted. Makes 6 servings.

SAUCY LAMB SHANKS

Sprinkle 4 *lamb shanks* (3½ to 4 pounds total) with some salt and pepper. In a large skillet brown lamb in 2 tablespoons hot *cooking oil*; drain off excess fat. In a mixing bowl stir together 1 cup finely chopped *onion*; 1 cup finely chopped *carrot*; 1 cup chopped *celery*; one 8-ounce can *tomato sauce*; 1 cup *dry red wine*; ½ cup *water*; 1 clove *garlic*, minced; 1 *bay leaf*; 1 teaspoon *salt*; and ⅛ teaspoon *pepper*. Pour over lamb. Cover; simmer for 1½ hours or till meat is tender.

Place lamb shanks atop *hot cooked noodles* on a serving platter. Remove bay leaf from tomato sauce mixture; discard. Skim excess fat from sauce; spoon sauce over lamb shanks and noodles. Makes 4 servings.

LAMB LOIN CHOPS WITH WALNUT GLAZE

 4 lamb loin chops, cut ¾ inch thick
 ¼ cup honey
 1 tablespoon lemon juice
 ¼ cup finely chopped walnuts
 2 tablespoons snipped parsley

Place lamb chops on an unheated rack in a broiler pan. Broil 3 inches from heat for 5 minutes. Season with salt and pepper. Turn; broil 5 to 6 minutes more. Combine honey and lemon juice; stir in walnuts and parsley. Spoon nut mixture over chops; broil 1 minute longer. Serves 4.

TONGUE AND LIMA SKILLET

 2 tablespoons chopped onion
 1 tablespoon butter or margarine
 1⅓ cups water
 1 10-ounce package frozen baby lima beans
 1 teaspoon instant beef bouillon granules
 1 teaspoon Worcestershire sauce
 ¼ teaspoon dried thyme, crushed
 ⅓ cup catsup
 1 tablespoon cornstarch
 12 ounces thinly sliced cooked tongue

In a 10-inch skillet cook onion in butter till tender but not brown. Stir in water, lima beans, bouillon granules, Worcestershire, and thyme. Bring to boiling. Reduce heat; simmer, covered, for 10 minutes. Stir catsup into cornstarch. Stir into *undrained* lima mixture. Cook and stir till thickened and bubbly. Cook and stir 1 to 2 minutes more. Stir in sliced tongue; heat through. Makes 4 servings.

PIES

Simplify your pie making with the following equipment: a pastry blender to cut in shortening, a rolling pin with a stockinette cover, a pastry cloth (to prevent pastry from sticking), and a pastry wheel to cut pastry strips. For baking pies, use a glass pie plate or a dull metal pie plate. (Shiny metal pans keep the crust from browning properly). Cool baked pies on a wire rack. The rack allows air to circulate under the pie and helps prevent the crust from becoming soggy.

The "secret" of pastry making is measuring accurately. Before measuring flour, stir it in the canister to lighten it. Then gently spoon the flour into a dry measure and level off the top with a metal spatula. (Too much flour makes the pastry tough.) To measure solid shortening, pack it into a dry measure, running a spatula through it to make sure there are no air pockets. (Too much shortening makes pastry greasy and crumbly.) To measure water for pastry, fill a measuring tablespoon to the top. Sprinkle 1 tablespoon water at a time over the flour-shortening mixture. (Too much water makes pastry tough and soggy.)

PASTRY FOR SINGLE-CRUST PIE

- 1¼ cups all-purpose flour
- ½ teaspoon salt
- ⅓ cup shortening or lard
- 3 to 4 tablespoons cold water

In a mixing bowl stir together flour and salt. Cut in shortening or lard till pieces are the size of small peas. Sprinkle *1 tablespoon* of the water over part of the mixture; gently toss with a fork. Push to side of bowl. Repeat till all is moistened. Form dough into a ball. On a lightly floured surface flatten dough with hands. Roll dough from center to edge, forming a circle about 12 inches in diameter. Wrap pastry around rolling pin. Unroll onto a 9-inch pie plate. Ease pastry into pie plate, being careful not to stretch pastry. Trim to ½ inch beyond edge of pie plate; fold under extra pastry. Make a fluted, rope-shaped, or scalloped edge. Do not prick pastry. Bake as directed in individual recipe.

Baked Pastry Shell: Prepare Pastry for Single-Crust Pie as above, *except* prick bottom and sides with tines of a fork. Bake in a 450° oven for 10 to 12 minutes or till golden. Cool on a wire rack.

Pastry for Double-Crust Pie: Prepare pastry for Single-Crust Pie as above, *except* use 2 cups *all-purpose flour*, 1 teaspoon *salt*, ⅔ cup *shortening or lard*, and 6 to 7 tablespoons *cold water*. Divide dough in half. Roll out half of dough as above. Fit into pie plate. Trim pastry even with rim. For top crust, roll out remaining dough. Cut slits for escape of steam. Place *desired pie filling* in pie shell. Top with pastry for top crust. Trim top crust ½ inch beyond edge of pie plate. Fold extra pastry under bottom crust; flute edge. Bake as directed in individual recipe.

Pastry for Lattice-Top Pie: Prepare Pastry for Double-Crust Pie as at left, *except* line a 9-inch plate with *half* of the pastry. Trim pastry to ½ inch beyond edge of pie plate. Turn filling into pastry-lined pie plate. Cut remaining pastry into ½-inch-wide strips. Weave strips atop filling to make a lattice crust. Press ends of strips into rim of crust. Fold bottom pastry over the lattice strips; seal and flute. Bake as directed in individual recipe.

APPLE CRUMBLE PIE

- 1 cup sugar
- 2 tablespoons all-purpose flour
- 1 teaspoon grated lemon peel
- 6 cups thinly sliced, peeled cooking apples (2 pounds)
- 3 tablespoons lemon juice
- Pastry for Single-Crust Pie (see recipe, page 110)
- ½ cup all-purpose flour
- ½ teaspoon ground cinnamon
- ¼ teaspoon ground ginger
- ⅛ teaspoon ground mace
- ¼ cup butter

Oven 375°

Combine ½ *cup* of the sugar, the 2 tablespoons flour, and the lemon peel. Sprinkle apple slices with lemon juice; add sugar mixture and toss to coat. Fill a pastry-lined 9-inch pie plate with apple mixture. Combine remaining ½ cup of sugar, the ½ cup flour, and the spices. Cut in the butter till crumbly; sprinkle mixture atop apples. Cover edge of pie with foil. Bake in a 375° oven for 30 minutes. Remove foil; bake for 30 minutes more or till topping is golden. Serve warm. Serves 8.

FRESH CHERRY PIE

> 4 cups fresh or frozen pitted tart red cherries (20 ounces)
> 1 cup sugar
> 3 tablespoons quick-cooking tapioca
> 1 tablespoon cherry brandy (optional)
> 1 teaspoon finely shredded lemon peel
> Pastry for Double-Crust Pie
>   (see recipe, page 110)
> 1 tablespoon butter or margarine   Oven 375°

In a large bowl combine cherries; sugar; tapioca; brandy, if desired; lemon peel; and ⅛ teaspoon *salt*. Let stand 20 minutes, stirring occasionally. Fill a pastry-lined 9-inch pie plate with cherry mixture; dot with butter or margarine. Adjust top crust. Seal and flute edge high. Cover edge of pie with foil. Bake in a 375° oven for 30 minutes. Remove foil; bake for 25 to 30 minutes more or till golden. Cool pie on a wire rack before serving. Serves 8.

APRICOT PIE

> 4 cups sliced, pitted fresh or frozen apricots
> 1 tablespoon lemon juice
> 1 cup sugar
> ¼ cup all-purpose flour
> ⅛ teaspoon ground nutmeg
> Pastry for Double-Crust Pie
>   (see recipe, page 110)
> 1 tablespoon butter or margarine   Oven 375°

In a large bowl sprinkle the apricots with lemon juice. Combine the sugar, flour, and nutmeg. Add sugar mixture to sliced apricots; toss to coat fruit. Fill a pastry-lined 9-inch pie plate with apricot mixture; dot with butter or margarine. Adjust top crust. Seal and flute edge. Cover edge of pie with foil. Bake in a 375° oven for 20 minutes. Remove foil; bake for 20 to 25 minutes more or till crust is golden. Cool on a wire rack before serving. Serves 8.

DEEP-DISH PEACH PIE

Pastry for Single-Crust Pie (see recipe, page 110)
- ¾ cup sugar
- 3 tablespoons all-purpose flour
- ¼ teaspoon ground nutmeg
- 6 cups peeled, thickly sliced fresh peaches (3 pounds)
- 3 tablespoons grenadine syrup
- 2 tablespoons lemon juice
- 2 tablespoons butter or margarine   Oven 375°

Prepare Pastry for Single-Crust Pie, *except* roll out into an even 9-inch or 11-inch circle (depending on dish size). Cut slits in pastry. Combine sugar, flour, and nutmeg. Add sugar mixture to peaches and toss to coat. Let stand 5 minutes. Stir in grenadine syrup and lemon juice. Turn mixture into a 1½-quart casserole or a deep 10-inch round baking dish, spreading peaches evenly; dot with butter. Place pastry over peach mixture in baking dish. Flute to side of dish but not over the edge. Cover edge with foil. Place dish on a baking sheet. Bake in a 375° oven for 25 minutes. Remove foil; bake for 30 to 35 minutes more or till crust is golden. Cool. Makes 8 servings.

FRESH PINEAPPLE PIE

- ¾ cup sugar
- 3 tablespoons quick-cooking tapioca
- 4 cups fresh pineapple cut into ¾-inch pieces
- 1 tablespoon lemon juice
- Pastry for Double-Crust Pie (see recipe, page 110)
- 1 tablespoon butter

Oven 375°

Stir together sugar, tapioca, and dash *salt*. In a large bowl combine pineapple pieces and lemon juice. Add sugar mixture to pineapple; toss to coat fruit. Let stand 15 minutes. Fill a pastry-lined 9-inch pie plate with pineapple mixture; dot with butter. Adjust top crust. Seal and flute edge. Cover edge of pie with foil. Bake in a 375° oven for 20 minutes. Remove foil; bake for 25 to 30 minutes more or till crust is golden. Cool pie thoroughly on a wire rack before serving. Makes 8 servings.

RAISIN CRISSCROSS PIE

- 1 cup packed brown sugar
- 2 tablespoons cornstarch
- 2 cups raisins
- ½ teaspoon finely shredded orange peel
- ½ cup orange juice
- ½ teaspoon finely shredded lemon peel
- 2 tablespoons lemon juice
- ½ cup chopped walnuts
- Pastry for Lattice-Top Pie (see recipe, page 111)

Oven 375°

In a saucepan combine brown sugar and cornstarch. Stir in raisins, orange peel and juice, lemon peel and juice, and 1⅓ cups cold *water*. Cook and stir over medium heat till thickened and bubbly; cook and stir 1 minute more. Remove from heat; stir in walnuts. Fill a pastry-lined 9-inch pie plate with raisin mixture. Adjust lattice crust; flute edge. Cover edge of pie with foil. Bake in a 375° oven for 20 minutes. Remove foil and bake about 20 minutes more or till crust is golden. Makes 8 servings.

STRAWBERRY GLACÉ PIE

- 6 cups fresh medium strawberries
- ¾ cup sugar
- 3 tablespoons cornstarch
- 5 drops red food coloring (optional)
- 1 9-inch Baked Pastry Shell
  (see recipe, page 110)

To prepare strawberry glaze, in a small saucepan crush *1 cup* of the smaller berries; add 1 cup *water*. Bring to boiling; simmer 2 minutes. Sieve berry mixture. In a saucepan combine sugar and cornstarch; stir in sieved berry mixture. Cook over medium heat, stirring constantly, till thickened and clear. Stir in red food coloring, if desired. Spread about ¼ *cup* of the strawberry glaze over bottom and sides of Baked Pastry Shell. Arrange *half* of the whole strawberries, stem end down, in pastry shell. Carefully spoon *half* of the remaining glaze over berries, thoroughly covering each berry. Arrange remaining strawberries, stem end down, atop first layer; spoon on remaining glaze, covering each berry. Chill pie at least 3 to 4 hours. If desired, garnish with unsweetened whipped cream. Makes 8 servings.

RHUBARB PIE

- 1¼ cups sugar
- ⅓ cup all-purpose flour
- 4 cups rhubarb cut into 1-inch pieces
  Pastry for Double-Crust Pie
  (see recipe, page 110)
- 2 tablespoons butter

Oven 375°

Stir together sugar, flour, and dash *salt*. Add sugar mixture to rhubarb pieces; toss to coat fruit. Let fruit mixture stand for 15 minutes. Fill a pastry-lined 9-inch pie plate with rhubarb mixture; dot with butter. Adjust top crust. Seal and flute edge. Cover edge of pie with foil. Bake in a 375° oven for 25 minutes. Remove foil and bake for 25 minutes more or till golden. Serve warm. Makes 8 servings.

Strawberry-Rhubarb Pie: Prepare Rhubarb Pie as above, *except* substitute 3 tablespoons quick-cooking *tapioca* for the flour and 3 cups *rhubarb* cut into ½-inch pieces plus 2 cups sliced fresh *strawberries* for the 4 cups rhubarb. Add ¼ teaspoon ground *nutmeg* to the tapioca mixture. Continue as directed.

LIME PARFAIT PIE

- 1 3-ounce package lime-flavored gelatin
- ½ cup boiling water
- ¾ teaspoon finely shredded lime peel
- ¼ cup lime juice
- 1 pint vanilla ice cream
- 1 cup whipping cream
- 1 9-inch Baked Pastry Shell
  (see recipe, page 110)

In a large bowl dissolve gelatin in boiling water. Stir in

lime peel and lime juice. Add ice cream by spoonfuls, stirring till melted. Chill till partially set (the consistency of unbeaten egg whites). Whip the 1 cup whipping cream; fold into lime mixture. Chill till mixture mounds when spooned. Turn into Baked Pastry Shell. Chill several hours or overnight till set. To serve, top with unsweetened whipped cream and maraschino cherries, if desired. Cover and chill to store. Makes 8 servings.

LEMON-CHESS PIE

Pastry for Single-Crust Pie (see recipe, page 110)
- 5 eggs
- 1½ cups sugar
- 1 cup light cream or milk
- ¼ cup butter or margarine, melted
- 1 teaspoon finely shredded lemon peel
- 2 tablespoons lemon juice
- 1 tablespoon all-purpose flour
- 1 tablespoon yellow cornmeal
- 1½ teaspoons vanilla

Oven 450°

Bake pastry in a 450° oven for 5 minutes. Cool on a wire rack. For filling, in a mixing bowl beat eggs till well combined. Stir in sugar, light cream or milk, butter or margarine, lemon peel and juice, flour, cornmeal, and vanilla. Mix well. Reduce oven temperature to 350°. Place pastry shell on oven rack. Pour filling into the partially baked pastry shell. Cover edge of pie with foil. Bake at 350° oven for 20 minutes. Remove foil from edge; bake for 20 to 25 minutes more or till a knife inserted off-center comes out clean. Cool pie on a wire rack. Cover and chill to store. Makes 8 servings.

CHOCOLATE CHIFFON PIE

- 1 envelope unflavored gelatin
- 3 egg yolks
- ⅓ cup sugar
- 1 teaspoon vanilla
- 2 squares (2 ounces) unsweetened chocolate
- 3 egg whites
- ½ cup sugar
- 1 9-inch Baked Pastry Shell
   (see recipe, page 110)

Soften gelatin in ¼ cup cold *water*. Beat egg yolks on high speed of electric mixer about 5 minutes or till thick and lemon colored. Gradually beat in ⅓ cup sugar; stir in vanilla and ¼ teaspoon *salt*. In a saucepan combine chocolate and ½ cup *water*. Cook and stir over low heat till chocolate melts. Add to gelatin; stir to dissolve gelatin. Gradually beat gelatin mixture into egg yolk mixture. Chill to the consistency of corn syrup, stirring occasionally. Immediately beat egg whites till soft peaks form. Gradually add ½ cup sugar, beating till stiff peaks form. When gelatin is partially set (the consistency of unbeaten egg whites) fold in stiff-beaten egg whites. Chill till mixture mounds when spooned. Turn into Baked Pastry Shell. Chill till set. Cover and chill. Serves 8.

POULTRY

Include poultry in your meals often to help stretch your food budget. Poultry is high in protein and other nutrients, but low in calories and fat. Choose a large chicken or turkey for a greater proportion of meat to bone, and more value for the money. You can use the leftovers in soups, salads, sandwiches, and casseroles.

CHICKEN PAPRIKASH

In a 12-inch skillet brown one 2½- to 3-pound *broiler-fryer chicken*, cut up, in 2 tablespoons hot *cooking oil* on all sides; season with salt and pepper. Remove browned chicken pieces from the skillet; set aside. Add 1 cup chopped *onion* to skillet; cook till tender but not brown. Stir in 1 tablespoon *paprika*. Return chicken to skillet, turning once to coat with paprika-onion mixture. Add ¼ cup *dry white wine* and ¼ cup *condensed chicken broth*. Bring to boiling. Reduce heat; cover and simmer 30 to 35 minutes or till chicken is tender. Remove chicken to a serving platter; keep warm. Boil skillet drippings about 2 minutes or till reduced to ½ cup liquid. Stir drippings into ½ cup *dairy sour cream*; return all to skillet. Heat through but *do not boil*. Pour sauce over chicken pieces. Serve over hot cooked *noodles*. Sprinkle with additional *paprika* and garnish with snipped *parsley*, if desired. Makes 6 servings.

OVEN-FRIED CHICKEN

- 3 cups corn flakes or ½ cup fine dry bread crumbs
- 1 2½- to 3-pound broiler-fryer chicken, cut up
- ¼ cup butter or margarine, melted

Oven 375°

For the crumb mixture, crush corn flakes finely enough to make 1 cup crumbs or use the ½ cup bread crumbs; set aside.

Rinse chicken pieces; pat dry with paper toweling. Season chicken with salt and pepper. Brush *each* piece with melted butter. Place crushed corn flakes or bread crumbs on a sheet of waxed paper; roll chicken in crumbs to coat. Arrange chicken, skin side up and so pieces don't touch, in a shallow baking pan. Bake in a 375° oven about 50 minutes or till tender. *Do not turn.* (Chicken is done when it is easily pierced with a fork. Test the thigh or breast at a point near the bone, since these parts require the most cooking time.) Serves 6.

Potato-Chip Chicken: Prepare Oven-Fried Chicken as above, *except* substitute 1½ cups crushed *potato chips* or *barbecue-flavored potato chips* for the crumb mixture. Do not season chicken with salt.

Parmesan Chicken: Prepare Oven-Fried Chicken as above, *except* substitute a mixture of ⅔ cup crushed *herb-seasoned stuffing mix*, ½ cup grated *Parmesan cheese*, and 3 tablespoons snipped *parsley* for the crumb mixture. Do not season chicken with salt.

Chicken Italiano: Prepare Oven-Fried Chicken as above, *except* substitute a mixture of 1 cup coarsely crushed 40% *bran flakes*, 2 teaspoons *Italian or onion salad dressing mix*, and ½ teaspoon *paprika* for the crumb mixture.

Curry and Parsley Chicken: Prepare Oven-Fried Chicken as at left, *except* substitute a mixture of ⅔ cup finely crushed *saltine crackers* (about 20 crackers), ¼ cup snipped *parsley*, 2 teaspoons *curry powder*, 1 teaspoon *onion salt*, and ⅛ teaspoon ground *ginger* for the crumb mixture. Do not season chicken with salt.

CORNMEAL BATTER FRIED CHICKEN

- 1 2½- to 3-pound broiler-fryer chicken, cut up
- ¾ cup all-purpose flour
- ½ cup yellow cornmeal
- 1 teaspoon salt
- ½ teaspoon baking powder
- ¼ teaspoon poultry seasoning
- ⅛ teaspoon garlic powder
- Dash cayenne
- 1 beaten egg
- 1 cup milk or 1¼ cup buttermilk
- 2 tablespoons cooking oil
- Cooking oil for deep-fat frying

In a large saucepan cover chicken with lightly salted water. Bring to boiling. Reduce heat. Cover and simmer for 20 minutes. Drain. Pat chicken dry with paper toweling.

In a mixing bowl combine flour, cornmeal, salt, baking powder, poultry seasoning, garlic powder, and cayenne. Stir together egg, milk, and 2 tablespoons oil. Combine with dry ingredients; beat till smooth. Dip chicken pieces, one at a time, into batter. Fry, a few at a time, in deep hot oil (365°) for 2 to 3 minutes or till golden. Drain well; keep warm while frying remaining chicken. Makes 6 servings.

CRISPY BAKED BARBECUED CHICKEN

- ½ cup fine dry bread crumbs
- 1 teaspoon brown sugar
- 1 teaspoon chili powder
- ½ teaspoon garlic powder
- ¼ teaspoon dry mustard
- ¼ teaspoon celery seed
- ⅛ teaspoon cayenne
- 1 2½- to 3-pound broiler-fryer chicken, cut up
- ¼ cup butter or margarine, melted   Oven 375°

Combine bread crumbs, brown sugar, chili powder, garlic powder, dry mustard, celery seed, and cayenne. Season chicken with salt and pepper. Brush *each* chicken piece with melted butter. Roll in crumb mixture to coat. Arrange chicken, skin side up and so pieces don't touch, in a shallow baking pan. Sprinkle with any remaining crumb mixture. Bake, uncovered, in a 375° oven about 50 minutes or till tender. *Do not turn*. Makes 6 servings.

CHICKEN A LA KING

For sauce, in a saucepan melt 6 tablespoons *butter or margarine*. Stir in ½ cup all-purpose *flour*, ¾ teaspoon *salt*, and ⅛ teaspoon *pepper*. Add 2 cups *milk*, 1 cup *water*, and 1 teaspoon *instant chicken bouillon granules* all at once. Cook and stir over medium heat till thickened and bubbly. Cook and stir 1 to 2 minutes more. Stir in 2 cups cubed cooked *chicken or turkey*; one 4-ounce can *mushroom stems and pieces*, drained; and ¼ cup chopped *pimiento*. Heat through. Serve spooned over *toast points, toasted English muffins, or baked patty shells*. Makes 4 servings.

Cheesy Chicken a la King: Prepare Chicken a la King as at left, *except* stir ½ cup shredded *American cheese* into the thickened sauce mixture. Cook and stir 2 minutes more. Continue as directed above.

CHICKEN SALTIMBOCCA

- 3 whole medium chicken breasts (2¼ pounds)
- 6 thin slices boiled ham
- 6 thin slices Swiss cheese
- 1 medium tomato, peeled, seeded, and chopped
- Dried sage, crushed
- ⅓ cup fine dry bread crumbs
- 2 tablespoons grated Parmesan cheese
- 2 tablespoons snipped parsley
- ⅛ cup butter or margarine, melted

Oven 350°

Skin, halve lengthwise, and bone chicken breasts. Place *1* piece of chicken, boned side up, between 2 pieces of clear plastic wrap. Working from the center to the edges, pound lightly with a meat mallet, forming a rectangle about ⅛ inch thick. Remove plastic wrap. Repeat with remaining chicken. Place a ham slice and a cheese slice on each cutlet, trimming to fit within ¼ inch of edges. Top with some chopped tomato; sprinkle lightly with sage. Fold in sides; roll up jelly roll style, pressing to seal. Combine bread crumbs, Parmesan cheese, and parsley. Dip chicken in butter, then roll in crumbs. Bake in a shallow baking pan in a 350° oven for 40 to 45 minutes. Remove to a serving platter. Stir mixture remaining in pan till smooth; spoon over chicken. Serves 6.

CHICKEN FRICASSEE

In a plastic bag combine ½ cup *all-purpose flour*, 1 teaspoon *salt*, 1 teaspoon *paprika*, and ¼ teaspoon *pepper*. Coat one 2½- to 3-pound *broiler-fryer chicken*, cut up, with flour mixture, 2 or 3 pieces at a time.

In a Dutch oven heat 2 tablespoons *cooking oil or shortening*. Brown chicken pieces over medium heat about 15 minutes, turning as necessary to brown evenly. Remove chicken. In the same Dutch oven cook ½ cup chopped *celery* and ½ cup chopped *onion* till tender but not brown. Drain fat, if necessary. Stir in one 10¾-ounce can of either condensed *cream of mushroom soup, cream of celery soup*, or *cream of chicken soup*; 1 cup *water*; 2 tablespoons chopped *pimiento*; 1 tablespoon *lemon juice*; and ½ teaspoon dried *rosemary or thyme*, crushed.

Return chicken to Dutch oven. Cover; cook over medium heat about 40 minutes or till chicken is tender; stirring occasionally. Serve with *hot cooked rice*. Makes 6 servings.

APRICOT CHICKEN

    3 whole medium chicken breasts
    1 21-ounce can apricot pie filling
    1 tablespoon lemon juice
    ½ teaspoon salt
    ½ teaspoon ground nutmeg
    ½ cup pecan halves
       Hot cooked rice   Oven 375°

Skin chicken breasts and halve lengthwise. Arrange in a 13×9×2-inch baking dish; sprinkle with a little salt and pepper. In a mixing bowl combine apricot pie filling, lemon juice, ½ teaspoon salt, and nutmeg. Stir in pecans. Pour apricot mixture over chicken pieces. Cover and bake in a 375° oven for 55 to 60 minutes or till chicken is tender. Arrange chicken on rice; spoon apricot mixture atop. Serves 6.

CHICKEN DIVAN

- 2 10-ounce packages frozen broccoli spears or two 8-ounce packages frozen cut asparagus
- ¼ cup butter or margarine
- ⅓ cup all-purpose flour
- ⅛ teaspoon ground nutmeg
- 1 cup light cream or milk
- 1 cup chicken broth
- ¼ cup dry white wine
- ⅓ cup shredded Swiss cheese
- 10 ounces sliced cooked chicken
- ¼ cup grated Parmesan cheese
  Paprika

Oven 350°

Cook vegetable according to package directions; drain. Arrange crosswise in a 12×7½×2-inch baking dish. For sauce, in a saucepan melt butter; stir in flour, nutmeg, ½ teaspoon *salt*, and ⅛ teaspoon *pepper*. Add cream or milk and broth all at once. Cook and stir till bubbly; continue cooking 1 to 2 minutes more. Stir in wine. Add Swiss cheese; stir till melted.

Pour *half* of the sauce over broccoli or asparagus. Top with chicken. Pour remaining sauce over all. Sprinkle Parmesan and paprika atop. Bake in a 350° oven for 20 minutes or till heated through. Broil 3 or 4 inches from heat 1 to 2 minutes or till golden. Serves 6.

OVEN-CRISPED ORANGE CHICKEN

- 1 beaten egg
- ½ of a 6-ounce can (⅓ cup) frozen orange juice concentrate, thawed
- 2 tablespoons soy sauce
- ½ cup fine dry bread crumbs
- 1 teaspoon paprika
- ¼ teaspoon salt
- 3 tablespoons butter or margarine
- 1 2½- to 3-pound broiler-fryer chicken, cut up

Oven 375°

Combine beaten egg, orange juice concentrate, and soy sauce; stir to mix well. In a small bowl thoroughly combine bread crumbs, paprika, and salt. Melt butter in a 13×9×2-inch baking pan. Dip chicken pieces in the orange-soy mixture, then coat with crumbs. Place chicken, skin side up and so pieces don't touch, in the baking pan. Sprinkle with any remaining crumb mixture. Bake, uncovered, in a 375° oven about 50 minutes or till tender. *Do not turn.* Makes 6 servings.

CROWD-SIZE CHICKEN BAKE

Oven 350°

Cook 16 ounces *medium noodles* (12 cups) according to package directions; drain well. In a large kettle melt ½ cup *butter or margarine*. Stir in ½ cup all-purpose *flour*, 1½ teaspoons *salt*, and ¼ teaspoon *white pepper*. Add 7 cups *milk* all at once. Cook and stir till thickened and bubbly. Cook and stir 1 to 2 minutes more. Stir in four 10½-ounce cans *chicken gravy*. Stir in 8 cups chopped *cooked chicken or turkey*; one 2-ounce jar sliced *pimiento*, drained and chopped; and cooked noodles. Divide between two 13×9×2-inch baking dishes. Bake, covered, in a 350° oven about 35 minutes.

Toss together 1 cup fine dry *bread crumbs* and ¼ cup *butter or margarine*, melted. Sprinkle atop casseroles. Bake, uncovered, 10 minutes. Makes 2 casseroles, 12 servings each.

CHICKEN WITH CURRANT GLAZE

- 1 3-pound whole roasting chicken
  Cooking oil
- ⅓ cup red currant or raspberry jelly
- 2 tablespoons lemon juice
- 1 tablespoon butter or margarine
- ¼ teaspoon salt
  Dash ground cinnamon
- 1 tablespoon cold water
- 2 teaspoons cornstarch   Oven 375°

Thoroughly rinse chicken; pat dry with paper toweling. Place chicken, breast side up, on a rack in a shallow roasting pan. Rub skin with oil. Insert a meat thermometer in the center of the inside thigh muscle but not touching bone. Roast, uncovered, in a 375° oven for 1¼ to 1½ hours or till thermometer registers 185°. In a small saucepan over low heat stir together jelly, lemon juice, butter or margarine, salt, and cinnamon till jelly melts. Combine water and cornstarch; stir into jelly mixture. Cook and stir over medium heat till thickened and bubbly. Cook and stir 1 to 2 minutes more. Brush on chicken several times during the last 15 minutes of roasting. Makes 6 servings.

CHICKEN-ASPARAGUS STACKS

In a saucepan cook ⅓ cup finely chopped *green onion* in 1 tablespoon *butter or margarine* till tender but not brown. Stir in one 10¾-ounce can *condensed cream of chicken soup*, ½ cup dairy *sour cream*, and ⅓ cup *milk*. Add 2 cups chopped *cooked chicken or turkey*. Heat through; *do not boil*.

Cook one 8-ounce package frozen *asparagus spears* according to package directions; drain. To serve, top *4 rusks*, with *half* of the chicken mixture. Top with *4 rusks*, asparagus, and remaining chicken mixture. Makes 4.

GLAZED CHICKEN AND RICE

For basting sauce, in a small saucepan combine ¼ cup *soy sauce*, 2 tablespoons *water*, 2 tablespoons *dry sherry*, 1 teaspoon *sugar*, and ½ teaspoon grated *gingerroot or* ⅛ teaspoon ground *ginger*. Boil gently, uncovered, for 1 minute. Set aside.

Halve or quarter one 2½- to 3-pound *broiler-fryer chicken*. Break wing, hip and drumstick joints so bird will remain flat. Twist wing tips under back. Brush poultry with *cooking oil*. Place chicken, skin side down, on an unheated rack in a broiler pan. Broil 5 to 6 inches from heat till poultry is tender, turning and brushing with cooking oil after half the cooking time. Brush poultry frequently with the basting sauce during the last 5 to 10 minutes, turning poultry as needed for even cooking.

Meanwhile, in a saucepan cook one 6-ounce package *long grain and wild rice mix* according to package directions. Stir in 1 cup fresh *or* canned *bean sprouts*, rinsed and drained; ¼ cup *green onion* bias-sliced into

1-inch lengths; and 2 tablespoons *butter or margarine*. Spoon rice mixture onto a warm serving platter; arrange poultry atop. Makes 6 servings.

POPOVER CHICKEN TARRAGON

Oven 350°

In a skillet brown one 2½- to 3-pound *broiler-fryer chicken*, cut up, in 2 tablespoons hot *cooking oil*; season with salt and pepper. Place in a well-greased 13×9×2-inch baking dish.

In a mixing bowl beat 3 *eggs*; add 1½ cups *milk* and 1 tablespoon *cooking oil*. Stir together 1½ cups all-purpose *flour*; ¾ to 1 teaspoon dried *tarragon*, crushed; and ¾ teaspoon *salt*. Add to egg mixture. Beat till smooth. Pour over chicken pieces in dish. Bake in a 350° oven for 55 to 60 minutes or till done. Serves 6.

ROAST TARRAGON CHICKEN

  1 **3-pound broiler-fryer chicken**
  2 **tablespoons lemon juice**
  2 **tablespoons butter or margarine**
1½ **teaspoons dried tarragon,
     crushed**   Oven 375°

Brush chicken with lemon juice inside and out; rub with ½ teaspoon *salt*. Skewer neck skin to back; tie legs to tail. Twist wings under back. Place, breast side up, on a rack in a shallow roasting pan. Melt butter; stir in tarragon. Brush over chicken. Roast, uncovered, in a 375° oven for 1¼ to 1½ hours or till done. Baste occasionally with drippings. Serves 6.

WILD-RICE-CHICKEN CASSEROLE

- 1 6-ounce package long grain and wild rice mix
- ½ cup chopped onion
- ½ cup chopped celery
- 2 tablespoons butter or margarine
- 1 10¾-ounce can condensed cream of mushroom soup
- ½ cup dairy sour cream
- ⅓ cup dry white wine
- ½ teaspoon curry powder
- 2 cups cubed cooked chicken or turkey

Oven 350°

Prepare rice mix according to package directions. Meanwhile, cook onion and celery in butter till tender. Stir in soup, sour cream, wine, and curry. Stir in chicken and cooked rice; turn into a 2-quart casserole or a 12×7½×2-inch baking dish. Bake, uncovered, in a 350° oven for 35 to 40 minutes. Stir before serving. Makes 4 to 6 servings.

CHICKEN LIVERS STROGANOFF

In a 10-inch skillet cook 3 slices *bacon* till crisp. Drain, reserving drippings in skillet. Crumble bacon; set aside. Cook 1 pound *chicken livers*, cut up, in drippings over medium heat 5 minutes or till slightly pink in center. Remove from skillet; keep warm.

In the same skillet cook 1½ cups sliced fresh *mushrooms* and ½ cup chopped *onion* 2 to 3 minutes. Remove from skillet. Add ½ cup dry *sherry*, ½ cup *water*, and ½ teaspoon *instant chicken bouillon gran-*

ules to skillet; bring to boiling. Cook, uncovered, till liquid is reduced to ½ cup. Stir together 1 tablespoon all-purpose *flour* and 1 cup dairy *sour cream*. Gradually stir hot liquid into sour cream mixture; return all to saucepan. Stir in crumbled bacon, chicken livers, and mushrooms and onion. Cook slowly till heated through; *do not boil*. Serve over *hot cooked noodles*. Sprinkle with snipped *parsley*, if desired. Serves 5 or 6.

HARVEST STUFFING

- 1 cup shredded carrot
- 1 cup chopped celery
- ½ cup chopped onion
- ½ cup butter or margarine
- 1 teaspoon ground sage or poultry seasoning
- ½ teaspoon salt
- ¼ teaspoon ground cinnamon
- 8 cups dry bread cubes
- 2 cups finely chopped, peeled apple
- ½ cup chopped walnuts
- ¼ cup wheat germ
- ½ to ¾ cup chicken broth

In a skillet cook carrot, celery, and onion in butter or margarine till tender but not brown. Stir in sage or poultry seasoning, salt, cinnamon, and ⅛ teaspoon *pepper*. In a large mixing bowl combine bread cubes, chopped apple, walnuts, and wheat germ. Add cooked vegetable mixture. Drizzle with enough chicken broth to moisten, tossing lightly. Use to stuff one 10-pound turkey. Makes 10 servings.

PAN GRAVY FOR ROAST POULTRY

Roast poultry
Hot drippings
¼ **cup all-purpose flour**
2 **cups water or chicken broth**

Remove roast poultry to a serving platter; keep warm. Leaving crusty bits in the roasting pan, pour pan drippings into a large measuring cup. Skim off and reserve fat from the pan drippings. (To skim the fat from the drippings, tilt the measuring cup and spoon off the oily liquid that rises to the top.) Return ¼ *cup* of the fat to the roasting pan; discard any remaining. Stir in flour. Cook and stir over medium heat till bubbly. Remove pan from heat. Add enough water or chicken broth to the drippings in the liquid measuring cup to equal 2 cups total liquid. Add all at once to flour mixture in pan. Cook and stir till thickened and bubbly. Cook and stir 1 to 2 minutes more. Season to taste. Makes 2 cups.

RICE, PASTA & CEREAL

Pasta

Dozens of varieties of pasta are available both at the supermarket and at import shops. Some pieces are especially suited for stuffing, while other pastas carry sauces and blend well in casseroles. The tiniest ones make a pleasant addition to soups.

For best eating, pasta should be cooked to the point Italians call *al dente* (to the tooth), when the pasta is still a bit firm, but no longer starchy. The best way to test pasta for doneness is to taste it. When done, drain it immediately to prevent further cooking.

If you need to keep pasta hot for a short time, return drained pasta to the empty cooking pan, add a little butter, and cover with a lid. For longer periods, place the colander of pasta over a pan containing a small amount of boiling water. Coat pasta with a little butter to keep it from sticking, and cover the colander.

Reduce the cooking time by ⅓ for pasta that will be cooked again in a casserole. Plan to serve about 1 ounce of pasta per serving for a side dish and about 2 ounces for a main dish.

SPAGHETTI WITH MARINARA SAUCE

- 1 large onion, chopped
- 2 medium carrots, finely chopped
- 2 cloves garlic, minced
- 2 tablespoons cooking oil
- 2 28-ounce cans tomatoes, cut up
- 1 teaspoon sugar
- 1 teaspoon salt
- 1 teaspoon dried oregano, crushed
- Dash pepper
- Dash crushed red pepper
- 8 ounces spaghetti, linguine, or other pasta

In a 3-quart saucepan cook onion, carrots, and garlic in hot oil till tender but not brown. Add *undrained* tomatoes, sugar, salt, oregano, pepper, and red pepper. Bring to boiling, reduce heat. Simmer, uncovered, for 45 to 60 minutes or to desired consistency.

Cook pasta in a large amount of boiling salted water till tender; drain well. Serve with tomato mixture. Makes 8 side-dish servings.

PASTA WITH PESTO

Try pesto on soups, vegetables, fish, or meats—
- 1 cup firmly packed snipped fresh basil
- ½ cup snipped parsley
- ½ cup grated Parmesan or Romano cheese (2 ounces)
- ¼ cup pine nuts, walnuts, or almonds
- 1 to 2 cloves garlic, quartered
- ⅓ cup olive oil or cooking oil
- 12 ounces spaghetti or other pasta

Place basil, parsley, cheese, nuts, garlic, and ¼ teaspoon *salt* in a blender container or food processor bowl. Cover and blend or process with several on/off turns till a paste forms. With machine running slowly, gradually add oil and blend or process to the consistency of soft butter. Refrigerate or freeze till ready to use.

Thaw pesto, if frozen. Cook pasta in a large amount of boiling salted water; drain well. Toss pesto with hot, cooked pasta; serve immediately. Makes 8 to 12 side-dish servings.

PASTA WITH CARBONARA SAUCE

- 4 eggs
- ¼ cup butter or margarine
- ¼ cup whipping cream
- ½ pound bacon, cut up
- 1 pound fettucine or spaghetti
- 1 cup grated Parmesan or Romano cheese (4 ounces)
- ¼ cup snipped parsley
- Pepper

Oven 250°

Let eggs; butter or margarine, and cream stand at room temperature for 2 to 3 hours. In a skillet cook bacon till brown. Remove bacon and drain on paper toweling.

Heat an ovenproof serving dish in a 250° oven. Meanwhile, beat together eggs and cream just till combined. Add pasta to a large amount of boiling salted water. Cook 10 to 12 minutes or till tender but firm; drain well.

Turn hot pasta into the heated serving dish; toss pasta with butter. Pour egg mixture over and toss till pasta is well coated. Add bacon, cheese, and parsley; toss to mix. Season to taste with pepper. Serve immediately. Makes 12 side-dish servings.

COTTAGE PASTA BAKE

    4 ounces fine noodles or medium noodles or
        elbow macaroni
    ¼ cup finely chopped onion
    1 clove garlic, minced
    1 tablespoon butter or margarine
 1½ cups cream-style cottage cheese
    1 cup dairy sour cream
    2 teaspoons poppy seed
    1 teaspoon Worcestershire sauce
    ½ teaspoon salt
        Dash pepper
        Dash bottled hot pepper sauce
        Paprika
        Grated Parmesan cheese
            (optional)

Oven 350°

Cook noodles in a large amount of boiling salted water till tender; drain well. Cook onion and garlic in hot butter till tender. Combine noodles and onion mixture. Stir in cottage cheese, sour cream, poppy seed, Worcestershire sauce, salt, pepper, and hot pepper sauce. Turn into a 10×6×2-inch baking dish. Bake in a 350° oven 25 to 30 minutes or till hot. Sprinkle with paprika; pass Parmesan cheese, if desired. Makes 6 side-dish servings.

Rice

Of the many types of rice, regular milled rice is the most familiar. Its husk is removed, then the grain is cleaned and polished. Parboiled rice keeps more of its nutrients because it is steamed under pressure before milling. Quick-cooking rice is precooked then dehydrated, and requires less time to cook. Brown rice retains more fiber and nutrients than milled rice because less of the bran is removed. It must cook longer and remains chewy when done, although quick-cooking brown rice also is available. Slender, dark grains of wild rice have a nutty flavor and require longer cooking, too.

To test rice for doneness, pinch a grain between your thumb and forefinger. If there's no hard core, the rice is done.

Cooked rice may be frozen or refrigerated. To reheat, add about 2 tablespoons water for each cup of cooked rice. Cover; simmer till hot.

COOKING RICE

- 2 cups cold water
- 1 cup long grain rice
- 1 tablespoon butter or margarine

In a saucepan mix water, rice, butter, and 1 teaspoon *salt*. Cover with a tight-fitting lid. Bring to boiling; reduce heat. Cook 15 minutes; do not lift cover. Remove from heat. Let stand, covered, for 10 minutes. Serves 6.

Microwave directions: In a 2-quart nonmetal casserole mix water, rice, and 1 teaspoon *salt*. Cook in a counter-top microwave oven on high power 6 minutes or till boiling. Stir; cover. Micro-cook 5 minutes. Stir; micro-cook, covered, 3 minutes longer. Stir; add butter. Cover and let stand several minutes.

Parsley Rice: Prepare rice as above, *except* stir ¼ cup snipped *parsley* into cooked rice.

Confetti Rice: Prepare rice as above, *except* cook one 10-ounce package frozen *mixed vegetables* according to package directions; drain well. Stir vegetables and ½ teaspoon dried *dillweed* into cooked rice. Serves 10.

Herbed Rice: Prepare rice as above, *except* before cooking add 2 teaspoons instant *chicken bouillon granules* and 1 teaspoon dried *thyme*, crushed; decrease salt to ½ teaspoon.

Note: Prepare a rice ring with any above variation by pressing hot rice into a buttered 5½-cup ring mold. Unmold at once.

MUSHROOM-RICE BAKE

- 2 cups sliced fresh mushrooms
- ¼ cup chopped onion
- 2 tablespoons butter or margarine
- 2 eggs
- 2 3-ounce packages cream cheese, softened
- 1 13-ounce can evaporated milk
- 3 cups cooked rice
- ¼ cup snipped parsley
- 1 teaspoon salt

Oven 350°

In a skillet cook mushrooms and onion in butter or margarine till onion is tender but not brown. Beat together eggs and cream cheese till smooth. Stir in milk. Stir in cooked rice, parsley, salt, and cooked mushroom mixture. Turn mixture into a 10×6×2-inch baking dish. Bake, uncovered, in a 350° oven for 40 to 45 minutes or till a knife inserted off-center comes out clean. Let stand 10 minutes before serving. Makes 8 to 10 servings.

Mushroom-Cereal Bake: Prepare Mushroom-Rice Bake as above, *except* substitute 3 cups cooked *barley or bulgur* for the rice. Continue as directed.

CHINESE FRIED RICE

Use long grain, quick-cooking, or brown rice—
- 3 tablespoons cooking oil
- 2 beaten eggs
- ½ cup diced fully cooked ham or raw pork
- ¼ cup finely chopped fresh mushrooms
- ¼ cup thinly sliced green onion
- 4 cups cooked rice, chilled
- 3 tablespoons soy sauce

In a 10-inch skillet heat *1 tablespoon* of the oil. Add beaten eggs and cook without stirring till set. Invert skillet over a baking sheet to remove cooked eggs; cut them into short, narrow strips. In the same skillet heat the remaining oil. Cook ham or pork, mushrooms, and green onion in the hot oil for 4 minutes or till mushrooms and onion are tender. Stir in cooked rice and the egg strips; sprinkle with 3 tablespoons soy sauce. Heat through, tossing gently to coat with soy. Serve with additional soy sauce, if desired. Serves 4 to 6.

Cereal

Cereals provide B vitamins and iron for good health, and whole-grain cereals add fiber to the diet. When combined with milk, cereal also is an excellent source of low-fat protein.

Whether ready-to-eat or uncooked, store cereal in a tightly covered container in a cool, dry place. In general, 1 ounce of ready-to-eat cereal makes 1 serving. For cooked cereal, plan on 1 cup uncooked cereal for about 4 servings.

SPICED PORRIDGE

1½ cups milk
½ cup raisins or currants
1 tablespoon sugar
¼ teaspoon ground cinnamon
⅓ cup quick-cooking farina

In a saucepan bring milk to boiling. Stir in raisins or currants, sugar, cinnamon, and ¼ teaspoon *salt*. Slowly add farina, stirring constantly. Cook and stir just to boiling. Reduce heat; cook and stir for 30 seconds. Cover and remove from heat; let stand 1 minute. Spoon into bowls. If desired, top each serving with butter and sugar; pass cream. Serves 2.

GRITS

1 cup quick-cooking hominy grits
1 teaspoon salt

In a saucepan bring 4 cups *water* to boiling. Slowly add grits and salt, stirring constantly. Cook and stir till boiling. Reduce heat; cook and stir 5 to 6 minutes or till all water is absorbed and mixture is thick. Serve with butter or milk, if desired. Serves 4.

Southern Cheese Grits: Prepare Grits as above. Stir 1½ cups shredded *American cheese* and ½ cup *butter or margarine* into the hot grits till melted. Gradually stir about *1 cup* of the hot mixture into 2 beaten *eggs*; return all to saucepan. Turn into a greased 8×8×2-inch baking dish. Bake, uncovered, in a 325° oven for 35 minutes or till nearly set. Let stand 10 minutes. Makes 8 servings.

SALADS & DRESSINGS

Salad Basics

On the next several pages you'll find a variety of delectable recipes for great tossed salads, molded vegetables and fruit salads, main-dish salads, and salad dressings. Whatever role the salad plays in your meal, combine these salad-making basics with a little ingenuity to create a tantalizing salad.

Probably the most familiar salad is the tossed green salad. But that doesn't mean it has to be commonplace. You can introduce interesting tastes and textures by combining a variety of salad greens. Besides the Basic Salad Greens, Swiss chard, mustard greens, beet tops, kale leaves, fennel, and dandelion greens make good additions to mixed green salads. Use full-flavored greens in small amounts.

A vegetable salad works as an appetizer or a side dish; a fruit salad functions as anything from a first course to a dessert. Either salad can be tossed, layered, or arranged however you please. For even more variety, combine fruits and vegetables.

Vegetable Salads

GREEN GODDESS SALAD

- 1 medium head romaine, torn (6 cups)
- ½ medium head curly endive, torn (3 cups)
- 1 9-ounce package frozen artichoke hearts, cooked, drained, and cooled, or one 14-ounce can artichoke hearts, drained
- ½ cup sliced pitted ripe olives
- 2 medium tomatoes, cut into wedges
  Green Goddess Dressing (see recipe, page 154)

In a large salad bowl combine romaine, endive, artichoke hearts, ripe olives, and tomato wedges. Cover and chill. To serve, pour desired amount of Green Goddess Dressing over the salad. Toss lightly to coat vegetables. Makes 6 to 8 servings.

ZUCCHINI SALAD BOWL

- 3 cups torn iceberg lettuce
- 3 cups torn romaine
- 1 cup thinly sliced zucchini
- ½ cup sliced radishes
- ½ cup sliced fresh mushrooms
- ½ cup thinly sliced carrots
- 2 green onions, thinly sliced
  Italian Dressing (see recipe, page 154)

In a large salad bowl combine the first 7 ingredients. Sprinkle with a little salt and pepper. Toss; cover and chill. Pour Italian Dressing over salad; toss lightly to coat vegetables. Makes 6 servings.

SPINACH-ORANGE TOSS

  6 cups torn fresh spinach (8 ounces)
  1 11-ounce can mandarin orange sections, drained
  1 cup sliced fresh mushrooms
  3 tablespoons salad oil
  1 tablespoon lemon juice
½ teaspoon poppy seed
¼ teaspoon salt
¾ cup toasted slivered almonds

Place torn spinach in a large salad bowl. Add mandarin orange sections and sliced fresh mushrooms. Toss lightly; cover and chill.

For dressing, in a screw-top jar combine salad oil, lemon juice, poppy seed, and salt. Cover and shake well. Chill. Shake again and pour the dressing over the spinach-orange mixture. Toss salad lightly to coat. Sprinkle toasted almonds over top. Serve immediately. Makes 6 servings.

SOUR CREAM CUCUMBERS

  2 medium cucumbers, thinly sliced
  1 small onion, thinly sliced
½ cup dairy sour cream
  1 tablespoon vinegar
  1 teaspoon sugar
½ teaspoon salt

Combine the cucumbers and onion. Stir together sour cream, vinegar, sugar, and salt; toss with vegetables. Cover and chill, stirring occasionally. Makes 3 to 4 cups.

ORIENTAL VEGETABLE TOSS

- ⅓ cup salad oil
- ¼ cup vinegar
- 1 tablespoon sugar
- 1 tablespoon soy sauce
- ¼ teaspoon ground ginger
- 1 8-ounce can water chestnuts, drained and sliced
- 6 ounces fresh or frozen pea pods, thawed
- 4 cups sliced Chinese cabbage
- 3 cups torn leaf lettuce
- 1 cup fresh bean sprouts
- 1 cup sliced fresh mushrooms
- 2 tablespoons chopped pimiento

For dressing, in a screw-top jar combine salad oil, vinegar, sugar, soy sauce, and ginger. Cover and shake well. In a large salad bowl combine water chestnuts, pea pods, Chinese cabbage, leaf lettuce, bean sprouts, mushrooms, and pimiento. Pour dressing over salad; toss lightly to coat vegetables. Serves 8.

MARINATED THREE-BEAN SALAD

- 1 8½-ounce can lima beans
- 1 8-ounce can cut green beans
- 1 8-ounce can red kidney beans
- 1 medium onion, thinly sliced and separated into rings
- ½ cup chopped green pepper
- ⅔ cup vinegar
- ½ cup salad oil
- ¼ cup sugar
- 1 teaspoon celery seed

Drain the canned beans. In a large bowl combine the lima beans, green beans, red kidney beans, onion rings, and green pepper. In a screw-top jar combine vinegar, salad oil, sugar, and celery seed; cover and shake well. Pour vinegar mixture over vegetables and stir lightly. Cover and chill at least 6 hours or overnight, stirring occasionally. Drain before serving. Makes 6 to 8 servings.

Quick Three-Bean Salad: Prepare Marinated Three-Bean Salad as above, *except* substitute one 8-ounce bottle *Italian salad dressing* for the vinegar, salad oil, sugar, and celery seed. Continue as directed; marinate in refrigerator for 1 to 1½ hours. Drain before serving.

HOT FIVE-BEAN SALAD

- 8 slices bacon
- ⅔ cup sugar
- 2 tablespoons cornstarch
- ¾ cup vinegar
- ½ cup water
- 1 16-ounce can cut green beans
- 1 16-ounce can lima beans
- 1 16-ounce can cut wax beans
- 1 15½-ounce can red kidney beans
- 1 15-ounce can garbanzo beans

In a large skillet cook bacon till crisp; drain, reserving ¼ cup drippings in the skillet. Crumble bacon and set aside. Combine sugar, cornstarch, 1½ teaspoons *salt*, and dash *pepper*; stir into reserved drippings. Stir in vinegar and water; cook and stir till boiling. Drain all cans of beans; stir beans into the skillet. Cover and simmer for 15 to 20 minutes. Stir in crumbled bacon. Transfer to a serving dish. Makes 10 to 12 servings.

MOLDED SHRIMP SALAD

In a mixing bowl soften 1 envelope *unflavored gelatin* in ½ cup *cold water*. Let stand 5 minutes. In a saucepan bring one 10¾-ounce can *condensed tomato soup* to a boil; add gelatin mixture and stir to dissolve. Remove from heat; turn into a large mixer bowl. Add one 8-ounce package *cream cheese*, cubed and softened, to soup mixture. Beat with a rotary beater or electric mixer till smooth. Stir in 1 cup *mayonnaise or salad dressing*. Chill till partially set (the consistency of unbeaten egg whites).

Fold in one 4½-ounce can small *shrimp*, drained; ½ cup chopped *celery*; ⅓ cup chopped *green pepper*; ⅓ cup chopped *onion*; and ¼ cup drained sweet *pickle relish*. Pour into an 8×8×2-inch dish or pan, or nine ½-cup molds. Cover and chill till firm. To serve, cut into squares or unmold onto lettuce-lined salad plates. Makes 9 servings.

GAZPACHO SALAD

In a bowl combine 3 medium *tomatoes*, cut into eighths; 1 medium *cucumber*, thinly sliced; 1 medium *green pepper*, coarsely chopped; 2 small *onions*, sliced and separated into rings; and 3 tablespoons snipped *parsley*.

For dressing, in a screw-top jar combine ¼ cup *salad oil*; 2 tablespoons *lemon juice*; 1 tablespoon *white wine vinegar*; 1 teaspoon dried *basil*, crushed; 1 clove garlic, minced; ½ teaspoon *salt*; and a few drops bottled *hot pepper sauce*. Cover and shake well. Pour the dressing over the tomato mixture. Toss lightly to coat vegetables. Cover and chill for 2 to 3 hours, stirring occasionally. Serve with *plain croutons*, if desired. Makes 4 to 6 servings.

CREAMY COLESLAW

    4 cups shredded cabbage
    ½ cup shredded carrot
    ¼ cup finely chopped green pepper
    2 tablespoons finely chopped onion
    ½ cup mayonnaise or salad dressing
    1 tablespoon vinegar
    2 teaspoons sugar
    1 teaspoon celery seed
    ¼ teaspoon salt

In a large bowl combine the cabbage, carrot, green pepper, and onion. To prepare dressing, stir together mayonnaise or salad dressing, vinegar, sugar, celery seed, and salt. Pour the dressing over the cabbage mixture; toss lightly to coat vegetables. Cover and chill. Makes 8 servings.

COLESLAW VINAIGRETTE

    2 cups shredded cabbage
    ⅓ cup sliced green pepper
    ¼ cup snipped parsley
    3 tablespoons vinegar
    2 tablespoons sugar
    2 tablespoons salad oil
    2 hard-cooked eggs, chilled

In a bowl combine cabbage, green pepper, and parsley. Stir together vinegar, sugar, salad oil, and 1 teaspoon *salt* till sugar is dissolved. Pour vinegar mixture over vegetables; toss to coat. Cover and chill. Separate yolk from white of *1* of the hard-cooked eggs. Cut up white; toss with cabbage. Slice remaining egg; arrange atop salad. Sieve yolk over the egg slices. Serves 4.

Fruit Salads

APRICOT SOUFFLÉ SALAD

- 1   3-ounce package orange-flavored gelatin
- 1   cup boiling water
- ½ cup cold water
- 2   tablespoons lemon juice
- ⅓ cup mayonnaise or salad dressing
- 2   tablespoons finely chopped celery
- 4 or 5 apricots, peeled and sliced
- 1   medium apple, thinly sliced

In a mixing bowl dissolve gelatin in boiling water. Stir in cold water and lemon juice. Chill till partially set (the consistency of unbeaten egg whites); beat with a rotary beater till fluffy. Beat in mayonnaise or salad dressing. Fold in celery. Arrange apricot and apple slices in the bottom of a 5- to 5½-cup mold; carefully spoon in the whipped gelatin mixture. Chill till firm. Serves 4 to 6.

CIDER WALDORF MOLD

- 2   cups apple cider or apple juice
- 1   3-ounce package lemon-flavored gelatin
- 1   cup finely chopped apple
- ¼ cup finely chopped celery
- ¼ cup finely chopped pecans
  Lettuce
  Mayonnaise or salad dressing

In a saucepan bring *1 cup* of the apple cider to boiling. Dissolve gelatin in boiling cider, stirring constantly. Stir in the remaining apple cider. Chill till partially set (the consistency of unbeaten egg whites).

Fold in chopped apple, celery, and pecans. Pour into a 3-cup mold or spoon into 6 individual molds. Chill till firm. Unmold onto lettuce-lined plate(s). Serve with mayonnaise or salad dressing. Makes 6 servings.

CHERRY-LEMON RING

- 1 3-ounce package lemon-flavored gelatin
- 1 3-ounce package cherry-flavored gelatin
- 2 cups boiling water
- 1 16-ounce can pitted dark sweet cherries
- 1 8-ounce carton lemon yogurt

Dissolve lemon- and cherry-flavored gelatins in boiling water. Drain and halve cherries; reserve syrup. Add enough water to syrup to measure 1½ cups liquid; stir into gelatin mixture. Add lemon yogurt; beat with a rotary beater till smooth. Chill till partially set (the consistency of unbeaten egg whites). Fold in the halved cherries. Pour into a 5½-cup ring mold. Chill till firm. Makes 8 servings.

FIVE-CUP SALAD

- 1 11-ounce can mandarin orange sections, drained
- 1 8¼-ounce can pineapple chunks, drained
- 1 cup coconut
- 1 cup tiny marshmallows
- 1 cup dairy sour cream

In a bowl combine mandarin orange sections, pineapple chunks, coconut marshmallows, and sour cream. Cover and chill for several hours or overnight. Makes 6 to 8 servings.

FRUIT STRATA SALAD

- 3 cups shredded lettuce
- 1 honeydew melon, peeled, seeded, and cubed
- 1 20-ounce can pineapple chunks, drained
- 1 pint strawberries, halved
- 1 large banana, sliced
- 1 8-ounce carton pineapple, lemon, or vanilla yogurt
- ½ cup shredded Gruyère or Swiss cheese (2 ounces)

In a large salad bowl place *half* of the lettuce. Layer fruits atop lettuce. Top with remaining lettuce. Spread yogurt over top; sprinkle with shredded cheese. Cover and chill 2 to 3 hours. Toss gently to serve. Makes 12 servings.

Main-Dish Salads

SHRIMP-AVOCADO SALAD

- 1 small avocado, peeled, seeded, and cut up
- ½ cup buttermilk
- 1 3-ounce package cream cheese
- 1 tablespoon lemon juice
- 1 small clove garlic
- ¼ teaspoon bottled hot pepper sauce
- 6 cups torn lettuce
- 1 pound shelled shrimp, cooked and drained
- 18 cherry tomatoes, halved
- 4 ounces Swiss cheese, cut into julienne strips

In a blender container place the first 6 ingredients and ½ teaspoon *salt*; cover and blend till smooth. Arrange lettuce in a salad bowl. Arrange shrimp, tomatoes, and cheese atop. Sprinkle with a little pepper. Toss with avocado mixture to serve. Makes 6 servings.

GREEK SALAD

- 1 head curly endive, torn (6 cups)
- ½ medium head iceberg lettuce, torn (3 cups)
- 10 ounces cooked lamb or beef, cut into julienne strips (2 cups)
- 2 tomatoes, peeled and chopped
- ¾ cup cubed feta cheese
- ¼ cup sliced pitted ripe olives
- ¼ cup sliced green onion
- ⅔ cup olive oil or salad oil
- ⅓ cup white wine vinegar
- ½ teaspoon salt
- ¼ teaspoon dried oregano, crushed
- 1 2-ounce can anchovy fillets, drained

In a mixing bowl toss together endive and lettuce; mound onto 6 individual salad plates. Arrange lamb or beef, tomatoes, feta cheese, olives, and onion atop greens. To make dressing, in a screw-top jar combine oil, vinegar, salt, oregano, and ⅛ teaspoon *pepper*. Cover; shake well to mix. Pour dressing over salads. Top salads with the anchovy fillets. Serves 6.

MEATLESS MEAL-IN-A-BOWL

  4 hard-cooked eggs, chilled
  4 cups torn fresh spinach
  1 15-ounce can garbanzo beans, drained
  1 cup cauliflower flowerets
  1 cup sliced fresh mushrooms
  1 cup cherry tomatoes, halved
  1 small cucumber, thinly sliced
  ½ small red onion, thinly sliced and
     separated into rings
  ½ cup coarsely chopped walnuts
  1 cup Avocado Dressing (see recipe, page 153)

Slice 3 of the hard-cooked eggs. Cut the remaining egg into wedges; set aside.

In a salad bowl combine torn spinach, beans, cauliflower flowerets, mushrooms, tomatoes, cucumber, onion, walnuts, and the sliced hard-cooked eggs. Pour Avocado Dressing over salad; toss to coat. Garnish with the hard-cooked egg wedges. Makes 6 servings.

CHEF'S SALAD

  1 clove garlic, halved
  6 cups torn iceberg lettuce
  3 cups torn romaine
  8 ounces Swiss or cheddar cheese
  6 ounces fully cooked ham or cooked beef
  6 ounces cooked chicken or turkey
  4 hard-cooked eggs, sliced
  3 medium tomatoes, cut into wedges
  2 small green peppers, cut into rings and
     quartered
    Salad dressing

Rub 6 large individual salad bowls with the cut surface of garlic clove. Place torn lettuce and romaine in salad bowls. Cut cheese, ham or beef, and chicken or turkey into julienne strips. Arrange cheese, meats, eggs, tomatoes, and green pepper over the greens. Serve with a salad dressing. Serves 6.

SCALLOP TOSS

Cook one 12-ounce package frozen *scallops* according to package directions; drain. Halve any large scallops. In a bowl marinate scallops in ½ cup *Russian Dressing* (see recipe, page 154) in the refrigerator for 30 minutes or till thoroughly chilled.

Rub a large salad bowl with the cut side of 1 clove *garlic*, halved; discard. Add 2 cups torn *iceberg lettuce*; 2 cups torn *romaine*; 2 cups torn fresh *spinach*; 3 hard-cooked *eggs*, chilled and quartered; ½ cup chopped *celery*; and 6 ounces *mozzarella cheese*, cut into julienne strips. Toss lightly to mix. Add the chilled scallop mixture; toss to coat. Makes 6 servings.

Salad Dressings

AVOCADO DRESSING

Combine ¾ cup *dairy sour cream*, ⅓ cup *milk*, 1 tablespoon *lemon juice*, ½ teaspoon *celery salt*, and a few dashes bottled *hot pepper sauce*. Stir in 1 large *avocado*, seeded, peeled, and mashed. If necessary, stir in additional milk to achieve desired serving consistency. Cover and refrigerate and use within a few hours to prevent discoloration. Makes about 1⅔ cups dressing.

154 Salads & Dressings

ITALIAN DRESSING

In a screw-top jar combine 1⅓ cups *salad oil*; ½ cup *vinegar*; ¼ cup grated *Parmesan cheese*, if desired; 1 tablespoon *sugar*; 2 teaspoons *salt*; 1 teaspoon *celery salt*; ½ teaspoon *white pepper*; ½ teaspoon *dry mustard*; ¼ teaspoon *paprika*; and 1 clove *garlic*, minced. Cover; shake well to mix. Chill. Shake again just before serving. Makes 1¾ cups.

FRENCH DRESSING

In a screw-top jar combine ½ cup *salad oil*, 2 tablespoons *vinegar*, 2 tablespoons *lemon juice*, 1 teaspoon *sugar*, ¾ teaspoon *dry mustard*, ½ teaspoon *salt*, ⅛ teaspoon *paprika*, and dash ground *red pepper*. Cover; shake well. Chill. Shake before serving. Makes ¾ cup.

GREEN GODDESS DRESSING

In a blender container combine 1 cup loosely packed *parsley leaves*; ½ cup *mayonnaise*; ½ cup *dairy sour cream*; 1 *green onion*, cut up; 2 tablespoons *tarragon vinegar*; 1 tablespoon *anchovy paste*; ½ teaspoon dried *basil*, crushed; and ¼ teaspoon *sugar*. Cover; blend till smooth. Store in a tightly covered jar in the refrigerator. Makes 1¼ cups.

RUSSIAN DRESSING

In a screw-top jar combine ⅔ cup *salad oil*, ½ cup *catsup*, ¼ cup *sugar*, 3 tablespoons *lemon juice*, 2 tablespoons *Worcestershire sauce*, 2 tablespoons *vinegar*, 2 tablespoons *water*, 1 tablespoon grated *onion*, ½ teaspoon *salt*, and ½ teaspoon *paprika*. Cover; shake. Chill. Shake before serving. Makes 1¾ cups.

SAUCES & RELISHES

Sauces

Sauces are made by many methods, but egg yolk-, cornstarch-, or flour-thickened sauces are considered to be the most difficult. You can avoid the pitfalls of these thickened sauces by faithfully following the directions. Prevent lumps in cornstarch- or flour-thickened sauces by stirring constantly during cooking. If you must leave the sauce for a few seconds, remove it from the heat while you're gone. Any lumps that might form usually can be removed by beating the sauce with a wire whisk or a rotary beater.

Eggs will not tolerate high temperatures or long cooking times. So egg-yolk-thickened sauces are best cooked in the top of a double boiler over—but not touching—boiling water. Add egg yolks by first stirring some of the hot mixture into the beaten egg yolks and then returning it all to the hot mixture in the double boiler. Never let a sauce boil after egg yolks have been added.

WHITE SAUCE

Medium White Sauce:
    2 tablespoons butter or margarine
    2 tablespoons all-purpose flour
    ¼ teaspoon salt
    Dash pepper
    1 cup milk

Thin White Sauce:
    1 tablespoon butter or margarine
    1 tablespoon all-purpose flour
    ¼ teaspoon salt
    Dash pepper
    1 cup milk

In a small saucepan melt butter or margarine. Stir in flour, salt, and pepper. Add milk all at once. Cook and stir over medium heat till thickened and bubbly. Cook and stir 1 to 2 minutes more. Makes about 1 cup.

Almond Sauce: Prepare Medium White Sauce as above, *except* toast ¼ cup slivered *almonds* in the melted butter. Add 1 teaspoon instant *chicken bouillon granules*. Continue as directed. Serve with vegetables or fish.

Cheese Sauce: Prepare Medium White Sauce as above, *except* add ¼ cup additional *milk*. Continue as directed. Over low heat stir 1 cup shredded *cheddar, Swiss, American, or Gruyère cheese* into the cooked sauce, stirring to melt. Serve with vegetables.

Confetti Sauce: Prepare Medium White Sauce as above, *except* stir in 2 tablespoons finely chopped *green pepper or parsley*, 1 tablespoon finely chopped pitted black *or* green *olives*, and 1 tablespoon finely chopped *pimiento*. Serve with vegetables, beef, or fish.

Herb-Garlic Sauce: Prepare Medium White Sauce

as at left, *except* cook 1 clove *garlic*, minced, in the butter or margarine for 1 minute. Continue as directed. Stir in ½ teaspoon dried *basil*, crushed, and ½ teaspoon dried *tarragon*, crushed, into the cooked sauce. Serve with vegetables.

Lemon-Chive Sauce: Prepare Medium White Sauce as on previous page, except stir in 1 tablespoon snipped *chives* and 2 teaspoons *lemon juice*. Serve with vegetables or fish.

Sherry Sauce: Prepare Medium White Sauce as on previous page, *except* stir in 2 tablespoons *dry sherry*. Cook 1 minute more. Serve with fish or veal.

CLASSIC HOLLANDAISE SAUCE

- 4 **egg yolks**
- ½ **cup butter or margarine, cut into thirds and at room temperature**
- 2 **to 3 tablespoons lemon juice**
- **Dash salt**
- **Dash white pepper**

Place egg yolks and ⅓ of the butter in the top of a double boiler. Cook, stirring rapidly, over boiling water till butter melts. (Water in the bottom of the double boiler should not touch the top pan.) Add ⅓ more of the butter and continue stirring rapidly. As butter melts and mixture thickens, add the remaining butter, stirring constantly. When butter is melted, remove pan from water; stir rapidly for 2 more minutes. Stir in lemon juice, 1 teaspoon at a time; stir in salt and white pepper. Heat again over boiling water, stirring constantly, for 2 to 3 minutes or till thickened. Remove at once from heat. If sauce curdles, immediately beat in 1 to 2 tablespoons *boiling water*. Serve with vegetables, poultry, fish, or eggs. Makes about 1 cup.

FRESH MINT SAUCE

- 1½ teaspoons cornstarch
- ¼ cup cold water
- ¼ cup snipped fresh mint leaves
- 3 tablespoons light corn syrup
- 1 tablespoon lemon juice
- 1 drop green food coloring (optional)

In a small saucepan combine cornstarch and cold water; stir in mint leaves, corn syrup, and lemon juice. Cook and stir till thickened and bubbly. Cook and stir 1 to 2 minutes more. Strain. If desired, stir in green food coloring. Serve with lamb or pork. Makes about ½ cup.

SAUCE PROVENÇALE

- 4 small tomatoes, peeled, seeded, and cut up (1 pound)
- ½ teaspoon sugar
- ¼ cup sliced green onion
- 1 clove garlic, minced
- 2 tablespoons butter or margarine
- ½ cup dry white wine
- 6 tablespoons butter or margarine
- 2 tablespoons snipped parsley

Sprinkle tomatoes with sugar; set aside. In a medium saucepan cook onion and garlic in the 2 tablespoons butter or margarine till tender but not brown. Add wine; cook over high heat, stirring occasionally, about 3 minutes or till liquid is slightly reduced. Stir in tomatoes, the 6 tablespoons butter or margarine, and parsley; heat through. Serve with beef or pork. Makes about 2 cups.

FLUFFY HORSERADISH SAUCE

- ½ cup whipping cream
- 3 tablespoons prepared horseradish
- ⅛ teaspoon salt

Whip cream just to soft peaks; fold in horseradish and salt. Serve with beef, pork, burgers, ham, or vegetables. Makes about 1 cup.

BORDELAISE SAUCE

- ½ cup dry red wine
- 1 tablespoon chopped shallot or onion
- ½ teaspoon dried thyme or tarragon, crushed
- 1 small bay leaf
- 1 14½-ounce can beef broth
- 2 tablespoons cornstarch
- 1 tablespoon butter or margarine
- 1 tablespoon lemon juice
- 1 teaspoon snipped parsley
- ⅛ teaspoon pepper

In a small saucepan combine wine, shallot or onion, thyme or tarragon, and bay leaf; bring to boiling. Reduce heat and simmer briskly, uncovered, for 5 minutes or till mixture is reduced by half volume (measure depth with a ruler at start and end of simmering time). Remove bay leaf. Combine the beef broth and cornstarch; stir into wine mixture. Cook and stir till thickened and bubbly. Cook and stir 1 to 2 minutes more. Add butter or margarine, lemon juice, parsley, and pepper; reduce heat and simmer, covered, for 5 minutes. Serve with beef, veal, or poultry. Makes about 2 cups.

MOCK HOLLANDAISE SAUCE

- ¼ cup dairy sour cream
- ¼ cup mayonnaise or salad dressing
- 1 teaspoon lemon juice
- ½ teaspoon prepared mustard

In a small saucepan combine sour cream, mayonnaise or salad dressing, lemon juice, and mustard. Cook and stir over low heat till heated through. (*Do not boil.*) Serve with vegetables. Makes about ½ cup.

TANGY CRANBERRY SAUCE

- 1 16-ounce can jellied cranberry sauce
- ⅓ cup steak sauce
- 1 tablespoon brown sugar
- 1 tablespoon cooking oil
- 2 teaspoons prepared mustard

In a mixer bowl combine cranberry sauce, steak sauce, brown sugar, oil, and mustard. Using an electric mixer or rotary beater, beat till smooth. Serve sauce warm or chilled with hamburgers, ham, pork, or poultry. Makes about 2 cups.

EASY BARBECUE SAUCE

- 1 14-ounce bottle hot-style catsup or one 12-ounce bottle chili sauce
- 3 tablespoons vinegar
- 1 teaspoon paprika
- ¾ teaspoon garlic powder

In a bowl combine catsup or chili sauce, vinegar, paprika, and garlic powder. Cover; chill for several hours. Use to baste burgers or beef during the last 10 minutes of barbecuing. Makes about 1½ cups.

TARTAR SAUCE

- 1 cup mayonnaise or salad dressing
- ¼ cup finely chopped dill pickle, finely chopped sweet pickle, or sweet pickle relish, drained
- 1 tablespoon finely chopped onion
- 1 tablespoon snipped parsley
- 1 tablespoon chopped pimiento
- 1 teaspoon lemon juice

In a bowl combine mayonnaise, pickle or pickle relish, onion, parsley, pimiento, and lemon juice. Cover and chill for several hours. Serve with fish or seafood. Makes about 1 cup.

Relishes

CRANBERRY-ORANGE RELISH

- 2 medium oranges
- 4 cups fresh cranberries (1 pound)
- 2 cups sugar
- ¼ cup finely chopped walnuts

With a vegetable peeler, remove the orange portion of the peel of one orange; set aside. Completely peel and section both oranges. Using a food grinder with a coarse blade or a food processor, grind reserved orange peel, orange sections, and cranberries. Stir in sugar and nuts. Chill for several hours. Serve with poultry or ham. Makes about 3½ cups.

FRESH CUCUMBER RELISH

- 3 **medium cucumbers (1½ pounds)**
- ½ **medium onion**
- ¼ **cup vinegar**
- 1 **tablespoon sugar**
- ½ **teaspoon salt**
- ¼ **teaspoon dried dillweed**

Slice cucumbers in half lengthwise; scoop out seeds and discard. Grind cucumbers and onion using a food grinder with a coarse blade *or* finely chop by hand; drain. Stir in vinegar, sugar, salt, and dried dillweed. Chill for 8 hours or overnight. Serve on frankfurters or hamburgers. Makes about 4 cups.

CINNAMON APPLE RINGS

- ½ **cup red cinnamon candies**
- ¼ **cup sugar**
- 2 **cups water**
- 4 **small cooking apples, peeled (if desired), cored, and cut crosswise into ½-inch rings**

In a 10-inch skillet combine candies and sugar; add water. Cook and stir over medium heat till liquid boils. Add apple rings to candy mixture. Simmer gently, uncovered, for 15 to 20 minutes or till tender. Stir occasionally and spoon candy mixture over apples. Cool apple rings in candy mixture. Drain. Makes about 3 cups.

SOUPS & STEWS

BEEF BOURGUIGNONNE

Cut 3 slices *bacon* into small pieces. In a Dutch oven cook bacon till crisp; remove bacon and set aside. Add ¼ cup *cooking oil* to bacon drippings. Cut 3 pounds boneless *beef chuck* into 1-inch cubes. Combine ⅓ cup all-purpose *flour*, 2 teaspoons *salt*, and ¼ teaspoon *pepper*. Toss beef cubes with flour mixture to coat.

Cook *half* of the beef; 2 medium *onions*, chopped; and 1 clove *garlic*, minced, in the hot oil mixture till beef is brown. Remove; set aside. Cook remaining beef in hot oil mixture till brown. Drain off fat; return beef-onion mixture to Dutch oven. In a small saucepan heat ¼ cup *cognac or brandy*; set aflame and pour over beef. Stir in 1 cup *burgundy*, 1 cup *beef broth*, and 2 *bay leaves*. Bring to boiling; reduce heat. Cover; simmer 1 hour or till meat is nearly tender.

Add 8 small *carrots*, cut up, and ½ pound tiny *onions*. Cover; cook 20 minutes more. Add 16 whole fresh *mushrooms*; cook 10 minutes more. Remove bay leaves. Stir in bacon. Garnish with snipped *parsley*. Serve with hot, cooked *noodles*. Serves 10.

QUICK BEEF GOULASH STEW

In a large saucepan cook 1 pound *ground beef* and ½ cup chopped *onion* till meat is browned and onion is tender. Drain off fat. Stir in one 10¼-ounce can *beef gravy*; one 7½-ounce can *tomatoes*, cut up; ½ cup *water*; and 1 teaspoon *Worcestershire sauce*. Bring to boiling. Add one 10-ounce package frozen *peas and carrots* and 1 cup uncooked fine *noodles*. Return to boiling. Cover; simmer for 10 minutes or till vegetables and noodles are tender. Serves 4.

CIDER STEW

Cut 2 pounds *beef stew meat* into 1-inch cubes. Combine 3 tablespoons all-purpose *flour*, 2 teaspoons *salt*, ¼ teaspoon *pepper*, and ¼ teaspoon dried *thyme*, crushed. Coat meat with flour mixture. In a Dutch oven brown meat, half at a time, in 3 tablespoons hot *cooking oil*. Drain off fat. Return all meat to Dutch oven. Stir in 2 cups *apple cider or apple juice*, ½ cup *water*, and 1 to 2 tablespoons *vinegar*. Bring to boiling; reduce heat. Cover and simmer about 1¼ hours or till meat is nearly tender. Stir in 3 medium *potatoes*, peeled and quartered; 4 medium *carrots*, quartered; 2 medium *onions*, sliced; and 1 stalk *celery*, sliced. Cover; simmer 30 minutes more or till meat and vegetables are done. Serves 6 to 8.

MEATBALL STEW WITH SPINACH DUMPLINGS

In a mixing bowl combine 1 beaten *egg*, ¾ cup *soft bread crumbs* (1 slice), and 1 teaspoon *garlic salt*. Add 1 pound *ground beef*; mix well. Shape mixture into 1-inch meatballs. In a 12-inch skillet heat 1 tablespoon *cooking oil*; brown meatballs in hot oil. Stir in ½ cup chopped *onion*; cook 5 minutes. Drain off fat. Combine one 11-ounce can condensed *cheddar cheese soup* and 1 soup can (1¼ cups) *milk*; stir into skillet mixture. Cover; simmer 10 minutes. Stir in one 16-ounce can diced *beets*, drained, and one 10-ounce package frozen *brussels sprouts*. Cover; simmer 5 minutes more.

Meanwhile, in a bowl combine one 8-ounce can *spinach*, well drained and chopped; 1 cup packaged *biscuit mix*; and ¼ cup *milk*. Drop spinach mixture atop bubbling-hot soup mixture to make eight dumplings. Cover; simmer 10 minutes (do not lift lid). Makes 4 servings.

CREOLE GUMBO

In a large saucepan cook ½ cup chopped *onion* and 1 clove *garlic*, minced, in 3 tablespoons *butter or margarine* till onion is tender. Blend in 3 tablespoons all-purpose *flour*. Cook, stirring constantly, till flour is golden brown. Stir in one 16-ounce can *tomatoes*, cut up; 1½ cups *water*; ½ cup chopped *green pepper*; 2 *bay leaves*; 1 teaspoon dried *oregano*, crushed; 1 teaspoon dried *thyme*, crushed; ½ teaspoon *salt*; and ¼ to ½ teaspoon bottled *hot pepper sauce*. Bring to boiling; reduce heat. Cover; simmer for 20 minutes.

Remove bay leaves. Stir in 10 ounces fresh *or* frozen *okra*, cut up (2 cups). Bring mixture to boiling; reduce heat. Simmer for 5 minutes. Drain two 4½-ounce cans *shrimp*. Stir shrimp and one 7-ounce can *crab meat*, drained, flaked, and cartilage removed, into okra mixture; cook about 5 minutes or till heated through. Serve the gumbo mixture over *hot cooked rice* in soup plates. (Traditionally, rice is mounded in a heated soup plate and the gumbo is spooned around it.) Serves 6.

QUICK BEANS-AND-FRANKS SOUP

In a saucepan combine ¾ cup chopped *celery*, ¾ cup chopped *onion*, ½ cup *water*, ½ teaspoon *salt*, and dash *pepper*. Cook 10 minutes or till vegetables are tender. Stir in two 16-ounce cans *pork and beans in tomato sauce*; mash slightly. Stir in 2 cups *milk* and ¼ cup *chili sauce*. Stir in 12 ounces *frankfurters*, sliced; heat through. Makes 6 servings.

EASY PORK CASSOULET

Oven 350°

In a skillet cook ½ pound bulk *pork sausage*; 1 medium *onion*, sliced; and 1 clove *garlic*, minced, till meat is browned and onion is tender. Drain off fat. Add 1½ cups cubed fully cooked *ham*, 2 tablespoons snipped *parsley*, and 1 *bay leaf*; mix well. Stir in two 15-ounce cans *navy beans, undrained*; ¼ cup dry white *wine*; and dash ground *cloves*. Turn into a 1½-quart casserole. Bake, covered, in a 350° oven for 45 minutes. Remove bay leaf. Serves 6.

SPLIT PEA SOUP

Rinse 2¼ cups dry *green split peas* (1 pound). In a Dutch oven combine peas; 8 cups cold *water*; 1 teaspoon *instant chicken bouillon granules*; 1 meaty *ham bone* (1½ pounds); 1 medium *onion*, chopped; ¼ teaspoon *pepper*; and ¼ teaspoon dried *marjoram*, crushed. Bring to boiling; reduce heat. Cover; simmer for 1 hour. Stir occasionally. Remove ham bone; when cool enough to handle, cut off meat and coarsely chop. Discard bone. Return meat to soup; stir in 2 medium *carrots*, chopped, and 2 stalks *celery*, chopped. Cover; simmer 30 minutes more. Season. Serves 10.

LENTIL SOUP

Rinse 1 pound dry *lentils* (2⅓ cups). In a Dutch oven combine lentils; 8 cups *cold water*; one 16-ounce can *tomatoes*, cut up; 2 slices *bacon*, cut up; 1 medium *onion*, chopped (½ cup); 1 medium *carrot*, chopped (½ cup); 3 tablespoons snipped *parsley*; 2 tablespoons *wine vinegar*; 1 clove *garlic*, minced; 2½ teaspoons *salt*; ½ teaspoon dried *oregano*, crushed; and ¼ teaspoon *pepper*. Bring to boiling; reduce heat. Cover; simmer 45 minutes. Serves 8 to 10.

GERMAN SAUSAGE CHOWDER

- 1 pound fully cooked bratwurst or knackwurst, cut into ½-inch pieces (8 links)
- 2 medium potatoes, peeled and chopped (2 cups)
- 1 medium onion, chopped (½ cup)
- 1 small head cabbage, shredded (4 cups)
- 3 cups milk
- 3 tablespoons all-purpose flour
- 1 cup shredded Swiss cheese (4 ounces)
- Snipped parsley

In a large saucepan or Dutch oven combine sausage, potatoes, onion, 1½ teaspoons *salt*, and dash *pepper*. Add 2 cups *water*. Bring to boiling; reduce heat. Cover; simmer for 20 minutes or till potatoes are nearly tender. Stir in cabbage; cook 10 minutes more or till vegetables are tender. Stir in 2½ *cups* of the milk. Stir remaining ½ cup milk into flour; stir into soup. Cook and stir till thickened and bubbly. Stir in cheese till melted. Garnish with parsley. Makes 6 servings.

QUICK CHEESY TUNA SOUP

In a saucepan cook 2 tablespoons chopped *onion* in 2 tablespoons *butter or margarine* till tender but not brown. Stir in one 11-ounce can condensed *cheddar cheese soup*; gradually stir in ½ cup *milk*. Stir in one 16-ounce can *tomatoes*, cut up; one 6¾-ounce can *tuna*, drained and broken into chunks; 1 tablespoon snipped *parsley*; and dash *pepper*. Bring to boiling; reduce heat. Cover; simmer for 10 minutes. Makes 4 side-dish servings.

FRESH CORN CHOWDER

- 6 fresh medium ears of corn
- ¼ cup chopped onion
- 4 cups milk
- 2 tablespoons butter or margarine
- 3 tablespoons all-purpose flour
- 1 slightly beaten egg

Using a sharp knife, cut tips of corn kernels off cobs. Scrape cobs. In a saucepan combine the corn, onion, ½ cup *water*, and ½ teaspoon *salt*. Bring to boiling; reduce heat. Cover; simmer about 15 minutes or till corn is barely done, stirring occasionally. Stir in 3½ *cups* of the milk, the butter or margarine, 1 teaspoon *salt*, and ¼ teaspoon *pepper*.

Combine the remaining ½ cup milk and the flour. Add milk-flour mixture to corn mixture. Cook and stir till thickened and bubbly. Gradually stir about *1 cup* of the hot mixture into beaten egg. Return to hot mixture in saucepan. Cook over low heat for 2 minutes more, stirring constantly (*do not boil*). If desired, garnish soup with snipped chives and paprika or crumbled bacon. Serves 6.

HAM HODGEPODGE

In a Dutch oven combine 5 cups chopped *cabbage*; 6 large *carrots*, cut into 1-inch pieces (1 pound); 2 large *potatoes*, peeled and chopped (3 cups); 3 cups *water*; 2 cups diced *ham* (10 ounces); ½ cup chopped *onion*; ½ teaspoon *salt*; ½ teaspoon *seasoned salt*; and ⅛ teaspoon *pepper*. Bring to boiling; reduce heat. Cover; simmer 1 hour. Stir in one 15-ounce can *garbanzo beans, undrained*; cover and cook 10 to 15 minutes more. (Add more water, if needed.) Makes 6 to 8 servings.

SHRIMP-RICE SOUP

- 2 cups sliced fresh mushrooms
- ¼ cup sliced green onion
- 1 clove garlic, minced
- 2 tablespoons butter or margarine
- 4 cups chicken broth
- ¾ cup dry white wine
- ½ teaspoon dried thyme, crushed
- ½ cup long grain rice
- 2 tablespoons cornstarch
- 12 ounces fresh or frozen shelled shrimp
- 2 tablespoons snipped parsley

In a saucepan cook mushrooms, onion, and garlic in butter till onion is tender but not brown. Stir in broth, wine, and thyme. Bring to boiling; stir in rice. Reduce heat; cover and simmer for 15 minutes. Blend 2 tablespoons *cold water* into cornstarch; stir into hot broth mixture. Cook and stir till bubbly. Stir in shrimp. Bring to boiling; reduce heat. Cover; simmer 1 to 2 minutes more or till shrimp are done. Stir in parsley. Serves 6.

CREAM OF CHICKEN SOUP

- ¼ cup butter or margarine
- ¼ cup all-purpose flour
- ½ cup milk
- ½ cup light cream
- 3 cups chicken broth
- 1½ cups finely chopped cooked chicken
- Dash pepper

In a large saucepan melt butter or margarine; stir in flour. Stir in milk, cream, and broth. Cook and stir till mixture is slightly thickened and bubbly; reduce heat. Stir in chicken and pepper; heat through. Garnish with snipped chives and parsley, if desired. Makes 4 servings.

CHEESE SOUP

- 1 cup finely chopped carrot
- ¼ cup finely chopped celery
- ¼ cup finely chopped onion
- 1¾ cups chicken broth
- 2 cups milk
- ¼ cup all-purpose flour
- Dash paprika
- 1 cup shredded American cheese (4 ounces)

In a medium saucepan combine carrot, celery, and onion; add chicken broth. Heat to boiling; reduce heat. Cover; simmer for 15 minutes or till vegetables are done. Combine milk, flour, paprika, and dash *salt*; stir into chicken broth mixture. Cook and stir till thickened and bubbly. Add cheese, stirring till melted. Makes 4 to 6 servings.

FRENCH ONION SOUP

- 1½ pounds onions, thinly sliced (6 cups)
- ¼ cup butter or margarine
- 3 10½-ounce cans condensed beef broth
- 1 teaspoon Worcestershire sauce
- 6 to 8 slices French bread, toasted
- Shredded Swiss cheese

In a large saucepan cook onions, covered, in butter about 20 minutes or till tender. Add condensed beef broth, Worcestershire sauce, ¼ teaspoon *salt*, and dash *pepper*; bring to boiling. Sprinkle toasted bread with cheese; place under broiler till cheese is lightly browned. Ladle soup into bowls and float bread atop. (*Or*, place a bread slice on soup in each broiler-proof soup bowl; sprinkle with cheese. Broil till cheese is lightly browned.) Makes 6 to 8 servings.

OYSTER STEW

- 1 pint shucked oysters
- 2 cups milk
- 1 cup light cream
- Dash bottled hot pepper sauce (optional)
- Paprika
- Butter or margarine

In a medium saucepan combine the *undrained* oysters and ¾ teaspoon *salt*. Cook over medium heat about 5 minutes or till edges of oysters curl. Stir in milk, cream, and hot pepper sauce. Heat through. Season to taste with additional salt and pepper. Sprinkle *each* serving with paprika and top with a pat of butter or margarine. Makes 4 servings.

SHERRY-PEA SOUP ELEGANTE

- 1 11¼-ounce can condensed green pea soup
- 1 10¾-ounce can condensed cream of chicken soup
- 1 14½-ounce can beef broth (about 2 cups)
- 2 cups light cream or milk
- ¼ cup dry sherry
- 2 tablespoons butter or margarine

In a saucepan combine green pea and cream of chicken soups; stir in beef broth and light cream or milk. Cook and stir till heated through. Stir in sherry and butter or margarine; heat through. Makes 8 to 10 appetizer servings.

DILLED LAMB RAGOUT

Oven 375°

Cut 2 pounds boneless *lamb* into ¾-inch cubes. Combine ⅓ cup all-purpose *flour*, 1½ teaspoons *salt*, ½ teaspoon *dried dillweed*, and dash *pepper*. Coat lamb with flour mixture. In an oven-proof Dutch oven heat ¼ cup *cooking oil*; brown lamb, half at a time, in hot oil. Return all meat to pan. Stir in any remaining flour mixture. Stir in 2 cups *water*. Bake, covered, in a 375° oven for 45 minutes. Stir in one 10-ounce package frozen *peas*, 1 cup sliced *celery*, and ½ cup *rosé wine*. Cover and bake 45 minutes more. Skim off fat. Stir about *1 cup* of the hot mixture into 1 cup dairy *sour cream*; return to remaining hot mixture. Cook and stir on top of range till heated through (*do not boil*). Makes 6 servings.

VEGETABLES

From artichokes to zucchini, choose fresh, frozen, canned, or dried vegetables as versatile meal accompaniments.

CREAMED VEGETABLES

For sauce, in a saucepan melt 1 tablespoon *butter or margarine*; stir in 1 tablespoon all-purpose *flour*, ¼ teaspoon *salt*, and dash *pepper*. Add 1 cup *milk* all at once. Cook and stir over medium heat till thickened and bubbly. Cook and stir 1 to 2 minutes more. Add 3 cups *cooked or canned vegetables*, drained. Heat through. Makes 4 to 6 servings.

Scalloped Vegetables: Prepare Creamed Vegetables as above, *except* pour into a 1-quart casserole. Combine ¾ cup *soft bread crumbs* and 2 tablespoons melted *butter*; sprinkle atop. Bake, uncovered, in a 350° oven for 20 to 25 minutes. Makes 4 to 6 servings.

Au Gratin Vegetables: Prepare sauce for Creamed Vegetables as above, *except* stir in 1 cup shredded *American cheese* (4 ounces) till melted. Stir in vegetables. Pour into a 1-quart casserole. Combine ½ cup *fine dry bread crumbs* and 2 tablespoons melted *butter*; sprinkle atop. Bake, uncovered, in a 350° oven for 20 to 25 minutes. Makes 4 to 6 servings.

GLAZED CARROTS

　　6 **medium carrots (1 pound)**
　　2 **tablespoons butter or margarine**
　⅓ **cup packed brown sugar**
　　1 **tablespoon snipped parsley**

Cut carrots in half crosswise then lengthwise into 2 or 3 sticks. Simmer, covered, in a small amount of boiling salted water about 10 minutes or till crisp-tender. Drain.

Melt the butter; stir in brown sugar till dissolved. Add carrots. Cook over medium-low heat about 10 minutes, turning often. Sprinkle with snipped parsley. Makes 6 servings.

ARTICHOKES VELVET

　　2 **cups sliced fresh mushrooms**
　　2 **tablespoons butter or margarine**
　　2 **9-ounce packages frozen artichoke hearts, cooked and drained**
　　1 **1-ounce envelope chicken gravy mix**
　⅛ **teaspoon dried thyme, crushed**
　⅛ **teaspoon dried marjoram, crushed**
　　1 **cup shredded Swiss cheese**
　　1 **tablespoon dry white wine**　　　　　Oven 350°

Cook mushrooms in butter about 5 minutes or till tender. Combine mushrooms and artichokes in a 1½-quart casserole. Prepare gravy mix according to package directions. Remove from heat. Add herbs and ¾ *cup* of the cheese; stir till melted. Stir in wine. Pour over vegetables. Cover; bake in a 350° oven for 25 to 30 minutes. Sprinkle with remaining cheese; bake 2 to 3 minutes more or till melted. Serves 6 to 8.

BROCCOLI ORIENTAL

- 2 10-ounce packages frozen broccoli spears
- 1 tablespoon butter or margarine
- 1 tablespoon sugar
- 1 tablespoon soy sauce
- 2 teaspoons sesame seed, toasted

Cook broccoli according to package directions. Drain; keep warm. Combine butter, sugar, soy, and 1 tablespoon *water*; heat till butter melts. Pour over broccoli; top with seeds. Serves 6.

POTLUCK VEGETABLE CASSEROLE

- 1 17-ounce can whole kernel corn
- 1 10-ounce package frozen cauliflower, cooked
- 1 10-ounce package frozen cut broccoli, cooked
- 1 4-ounce can sliced mushrooms
- 1 17-ounce can cream-style corn
- 2 cups shredded Swiss cheese
- 1 10¾-ounce can condensed cream of celery soup
- 2 tablespoons butter
- 1½ cups soft rye or white bread crumbs

Oven 375°

Drain whole kernel corn, cooked cauliflower, cooked broccoli, and mushrooms. Cut up large pieces of cauliflower. Combine cream-style corn, cheese, and soup. Fold in drained vegetables. Turn into a 12×7½×2-inch baking dish. Melt butter; toss with crumbs. Sprinkle atop mixture. Bake, uncovered, in a 375° oven 30 to 35 minutes or till hot. Serves 12 to 15.

POTATO PATTIES

  2 **tablespoons finely chopped onion**
  ¼ **cup butter or margarine**
  3 **medium potatoes, cooked, mashed, and chilled (2 cups mashed)**
  1 **slightly beaten egg**
  ¼ **cup all-purpose flour**

In a 10-inch skillet cook onion in *1 tablespoon* of the butter. Drain onion, reserving drippings in skillet. Combine onion, mashed potatoes, and egg. Shape into six 3-inch patties. Dip in flour. Add the remaining *3 tablespoons* butter or shortening to skillet. Heat over medium heat. Add potato patties and cook about 5 minutes on each side or till browned. Serves 6.

OVEN-BROWNED POTATOES

Peel 4 or 5 medium *potatoes*. Quarter and cook in boiling salted water about 10 minutes; drain. About 40 minutes before roast is done, place potatoes in drippings around roast, turning to coat. If necessary, add ½ cup *water* to pan to make enough drippings.

PENNSYLVANIA RED CABBAGE

Heat 2 tablespoons *bacon drippings or cooking oil* in a skillet. Stir in ¼ cup packed *brown sugar*, ¼ cup *vinegar*, ¼ cup *water*, 1¼ teaspoons *salt*, ½ to 1 teaspoon *caraway seed*, and dash *pepper*. Add 4 cups shredded *red cabbage* and 2 cups cubed unpeeled *apple*, stirring to coat. Cover and cook over medium-low heat, stirring occasionally. For crisp cabbage, cook 15 minutes; for tender cabbage, cook about 30 minutes. Makes 5 or 6 servings.

CREAMED SPINACH WITH NUTMEG

1   10-ounce package frozen chopped spinach
1   tablespoon butter or margarine
½   cup milk
1½ teaspoons cornstarch
    Dash ground nutmeg

Cook frozen spinach according to package directions using ½ cup *water*. Remove from heat. *Do not drain.* Add butter. Stir milk into cornstarch and nutmeg; add to spinach. Cook and stir till thickened and bubbly. Cook and stir 1 to 2 minutes more. Serve in sauce dishes. Makes 4 servings.

MINTED NEW PEAS

½ cup chopped green onion
3 tablespoons butter or margarine
2 cups shelled peas or one 10-ounce package
   frozen peas
2 tablespoons water
1 tablespoon finely chopped fresh mint
   leaves or 1 teaspoon dried mint
1 teaspoon sugar
1 teaspoon lemon juice
¼ teaspoon salt
¼ teaspoon dried rosemary, crushed

Cook green onion in butter till tender. Add fresh or frozen peas, water, mint, sugar, lemon juice, salt, and rosemary. Cover and cook 10 to 12 minutes or till peas are just tender; add more water as necessary. Garnish with a lemon twist and fresh mint leaves, if desired. Serves 4.

PEA PODS WITH ALMONDS

Combine ½ cup *water*, 1 tablespoon *soy sauce*, 1½ teaspoons *cornstarch*, and 1 teaspoon instant *chicken bouillon granules*; set aside.

Melt 2 tablespoons *butter* in a 10-inch skillet. Add 2 tablespoons slivered *almonds*; stir-fry 2 minutes or till lightly browned. Add one 6-ounce package frozen *pea pods*; stir-fry 2 minutes more. Stir in one 4-ounce can sliced *mushrooms*, drained. Stir cornstarch mixture; add to pea pods in skillet. Cook and stir till thickened and bubbly. Cook and stir 1 to 2 minutes more. Serves 3 or 4.

CARROT-RICE BAKE

- 3 cups shredded carrots (1 pound)
- 1½ cups water
- ⅔ cup long grain rice
- ½ teaspoon salt
- 2 cups shredded American cheese (8 ounces)
- 1 cup milk
- 2 beaten eggs
- 2 tablespoons minced dried onion
- ¼ teaspoon pepper

Oven 350°

In a saucepan combine carrots, water, rice, and salt. Bring to boiling. Reduce heat and simmer, covered, about 15 minutes or till rice is done. Do not drain. Stir in 1½ *cups* of the shredded cheese, milk, eggs, onion, and pepper. Turn into a 10×6×2-inch baking dish. Bake, uncovered, in a 350° oven for 20 to 25 minutes. Top with remaining ½ cup shredded cheese. Return to oven about 2 minutes longer to melt cheese. Cut into squares. Serves 6.

EASY BAKED BEANS

Oven 350°

Cook 4 slices *bacon* till crisp. Remove bacon, reserving about 3 tablespoons drippings in skillet. Drain and crumble bacon; set aside. Cook ½ cup chopped *onion* in reserved drippings till tender. Stir in two 16-ounce cans *pork and beans in tomato sauce*, 2 tablespoons *brown sugar*, 2 tablespoons *catsup*, 1 tablespoon *Worcestershire sauce*, and 1 tablespoon *prepared mustard*. Turn into a 1½-quart casserole. Bake, uncovered, in a 350° oven for 1½ to 1¾ hours. Stir, top with bacon. Let stand a few minutes before serving. Makes 6 servings.

SESAME ASPARAGUS

- 2 8-ounce packages frozen cut asparagus
- 1 2½-ounce jar sliced mushrooms, drained
- 2 tablespoons butter or margarine
- 1 teaspoon lemon juice
- 1 teaspoon sesame seed, toasted

Cook frozen asparagus according to package directions. Drain well. Season to taste with salt and pepper. Gently stir in mushrooms, butter, and lemon juice. Cook until heated through. Turn mixture into a serving bowl; sprinkle with sesame seed. Makes 6 servings.

Microwave directions: Place frozen asparagus in a 1½-quart nonmetal casserole. Cook, covered, in a counter-top microwave oven on high power about 10 minutes or till tender, stirring twice. Drain well. Season. Gently stir in mushrooms, butter, and lemon juice. Micro-cook, covered, about 2 minutes or till heated through, stirring once. Turn into a serving bowl; sprinkle with sesame seed.

CREAMY CURRIED CORN

In a saucepan melt 3 tablespoons *butter*. Add 2 cups cut *fresh corn or* one 10-ounce package frozen *whole kernel corn*, 2 tablespoons chopped *green pepper*, 2 tablespoons chopped *onion*, ¼ to ½ teaspoon *curry powder*, ¼ teaspoon *salt*, and dash *pepper*. Cover; cook over medium heat 8 to 10 minutes or till corn is just tender. Add one 3-ounce package *cream cheese*, cut into cubes, and ⅓ cup *milk*; stir over low heat till combined. Makes 4 servings.

HERBED LIMA BEAN BAKE

  2 10-ounce packages frozen lima beans
¼ cup chopped onion
  3 tablespoons butter or margarine
  1 cup herb-seasoned stuffing mix
⅓ cup water
  1 cup dairy sour cream
  1 tablespoon all-purpose flour
⅔ cup milk
½ cup shredded American cheese (2 ounces)

Oven 350°

Cook lima beans according to package directions. Meanwhile, in a small saucepan cook onion in butter or margarine till tender. Add stuffing mix and water; toss to mix. Set aside. Drain lima beans. Combine sour cream and flour; stir in milk. Stir into beans along with cheese. Add about ⅔ of the stuffing mix mixture; mix well. Turn into a 1½-quart casserole; sprinkle with remaining stuffing mixture. Bake, uncovered, in a 350° oven for 18 to 20 minutes or till heated through. Makes 6 to 8 servings.

GREEN BEANS ESPECIAL

- 1 9-ounce package frozen French-style green beans or one 16-ounce can French-style green beans
- ¼ cup diced fully cooked ham
- 2 tablespoons finely chopped onion
- 1 tablespoon butter or margarine
- 1 small tomato, peeled, cored, and coarsely chopped

Cook frozen beans according to package directions; drain. (*Or*, drain canned beans.) In a saucepan cook ham and onion in butter, stirring occasionally, till onion is tender. Stir in drained cooked or canned beans, tomato, and dash *pepper*. Cover; heat through. Serves 4.

CORN CUSTARD PUDDING

- ⅓ cup finely chopped onion
- 1 tablespoon butter or margarine
- 1 17-ounce can whole kernel corn
- 3 slightly beaten eggs
- 1½ cups milk
- 1 teaspoon sugar

Oven 350°

In a small saucepan cook onion in butter till tender but not brown. Drain corn. In a bowl combine eggs, corn, milk, sugar, and 1 teaspoon *salt*. Add the onion mixture. Turn into an 8 × 1½-inch round baking dish. Place in a larger baking pan. Place on oven rack. Pour boiling water into larger baking pan to a depth of 1 inch. Bake, uncovered, in a 350° oven for 25 to 30 minutes or till a knife inserted near center comes out clean. Makes 6 servings.

MUSHROOMS ELEGANTE

Toss 3 cups sliced fresh *mushrooms* (8 ounces) and 2 tablespoons chopped *onion* with 1 tablespoon all-purpose *flour*. Cook mushrooms and onion in 3 tablespoons *butter or margarine*, covered, over low heat 8 to 10 minutes or till tender, stirring occasionally. Add 1 cup *light cream or milk*, 2 tablespoons grated *Parmesan cheese*, ⅛ teaspoon *salt*, and ⅛ teaspoon *pepper*. Cook and stir till slightly thickened and bubbly; cook 2 minutes more.

Stir about *1 cup* of the hot mixture into 2 beaten *egg yolks*; return to saucepan. Cook and stir 2 minutes more or just till bubbly. Remove from heat; stir in 1 tablespoon *lemon juice*. Serve in sauce dishes. Makes 4 servings.

CANDIED SQUASH RINGS

2 acorn squash
½ cup packed brown sugar
¼ cup butter or margarine
2 tablespoons water   Oven 350°

Cut squash crosswise into 1-inch-thick slices; discard seeds. Arrange in a single layer in a shallow baking pan. Season with salt and pepper. Cover; bake in a 350° oven about 40 minutes. In a saucepan combine brown sugar, butter, and water; cook and stir till bubbly. Spoon over squash. Continue baking, uncovered, about 15 minutes more or till squash is tender; baste often. Serves 4 to 6.

Microwave directions: Pierce squash with a metal skewer or long-tined fork in several places. Cook in a counter-top microwave oven on high power 8 to 10 minutes or till soft. Let stand 5 minutes. Cut crosswise into 1-inch-thick slices; discard seeds. Place squash in a 12×7½×2-inch nonmetal baking dish. Season. In a glass measuring cup combine remaining ingredients. Micro-cook 15 seconds. Spoon over squash. Cover with waxed paper. Micro-cook 3 to 5 minutes or till hot. Baste once.

SPICY STUFFED EGGPLANT

- 1 medium eggplant (about 1 pound)
- ⅓ cup chopped onion
- 1 clove garlic, minced
- 1 tablespoon snipped parsley
- 3 tablespoons butter or margarine
- ¾ cup soft bread crumbs
- ¼ cup chopped pitted ripe olives
- 2 tablespoons chopped canned green chili peppers
- 2 tablespoons cooking oil
- 2 tablespoons lemon juice
- ¼ teaspoon dried basil, crushed
- ¾ cup shredded provolone cheese
- 4 to 6 tomato slices

Oven 350°

Halve eggplant lengthwise; scoop out and reserve pulp, leaving a ¼-inch shell. Cook shells, covered, in enough boiling water to cover for 2 minutes or till tender; drain. Chop uncooked pulp finely. Cook pulp with onion, garlic, and parsley in butter till tender. Stir in bread crumbs, olives, chili peppers, oil, lemon juice, basil, and ¼ teaspoon *salt*. Stir in ½ *cup* of the cheese. Pile into shells. Bake, covered, in a 350° oven 20 minutes. Top with tomato slices; brush with *cooking oil*. Top with remaining cheese. Bake, uncovered, 5 to 10 minutes. Serves 4.

DILLY PANNED SUMMER SQUASH

- 1 pound zucchini or yellow crookneck squash
- 2 tablespoons butter or margarine
- 1 tablespoon snipped parsley
- ¼ teaspoon salt
- ¼ teaspoon dried dillweed
- Dash pepper

Slice unpeeled squash to make 3 cups. In a medium skillet melt butter or margarine. Add squash; sprinkle squash with parsley, salt, dillweed, and pepper. Cover and cook over medium-low heat 8 to 10 minutes or till tender, stirring frequently. Makes 3 or 4 servings.

FRESH TOMATO FIX-UPS

Broiled Tomatoes: Halve 3 large unpeeled ripe *tomatoes* or cut a slice from the tops of 6 medium unpeeled ripe *tomatoes*. Place, cut side up, in a shallow baking pan. Season with salt and pepper. If desired, sprinkle each with ⅛ to ¼ teaspoon dried *basil or thyme*, crushed, *or* 1 teaspoon snipped *fresh parsley or chives*. Dot each with about 1 teaspoon *butter or margarine*. Broil 3 inches from heat about 5 minutes or till heated through. Makes 6 servings.

Baked Tomatoes: Halve 3 large unpeeled ripe *tomatoes* or cut a slice from tops of 6 medium unpeeled ripe *tomatoes*. Place, cut side up, in a shallow baking pan. Season with salt and pepper. Combine ½ cup crushed *saltine crackers*, 2 tablespoons melted *butter*, and 1 teaspoon dried *basil*, crushed; sprinkle atop tomatoes. Bake, uncovered, in a 375° oven about 20 minutes. Serves 6.

INDEX

A
Acorn Squash, Grilled, 20
Almond Cookies, 59
Almond Sauce, 156
Anadama Bread, 31
Angel Cake, 44
Appetizers, 5-12
  Baked Ham-Stuffed Mushrooms, 6
  Blue Cheese Onion Dip, 12
  Cheese Ball, 8
  Cheese-Wine Log, 8
  Cocktail Meatballs, 9
  Creamy Dill Dip, 11
  Creamy Onion Dip, 12
  Crunch Party Mix, 11
  Egg Salad Triangles, 7
  Fluffy Fruit Dip, 12
  Oysters Rockefeller, 10
  Party Ham Sandwiches, 7
  Shrimp-Cucumber Appetizer Spread, 5
  Swiss Cheese-Ham Spread, 8
Apples
  Apple Crumble Pie, 111
  Apple-Peanut-Buttered Pork Steaks, 18
  Apple-Raisin Muffins, 33
  Baked Apples, 68
  Cinnamon Apple Rings, 162
  Fresh Fruit Crisp, 65
  Sausage- and Apple-Stuffed Squash, 105
Applesauce Spice Cake, 41
Apricots
  Apricot Chicken, 124
  Apricot-Filled Oatmeal Bars, 50
  Apricot-Ham Patties, 104
  Apricot Pie, 112
  Apricot Soufflé Salad, 148
  Apricot Swizzle, 24
Artichokes Velvet, 174
Asparagus
  Chicken-Asparagus Stacks, 128
  Chicken Divan, 125
  Sesame Asparagus, 179
Au Gratin Vegetables, 173
Avocado Dressing, 153

B
Baked Alaska, 70
Baked Beans, Easy, 179
Banana-Nut Muffins, 33
Barbecue Recipes, 13-22
  Apple-Peanut-Buttered Pork Steaks, 18
  Beef Teriyaki, 14
  Corn-Stuffed Pork Chops, 17
  Foil-Barbecued Shrimp, 19
  Glazed Ham Slice, 16
  Grilled Acorn Squash, 20
  Grilled Bread Fix-Ups, 21
  Grilled Salmon Steaks, 18
  Italian-Seasoned Vegetable Kebabs, 21
  Onion-Stuffed Steak, 15
  Pineapple-Glazed Chicken, 16
  Polish Sausage-Krauters, 19
  Quick Garlic Cubed Steaks, 14
  Wine-Sauced Shoulder Chops, 20
Barbecue Sauce, Easy, 160
Batter Rolls, 28
Beans
  Easy Baked Beans, 179
  Green Beans Especial, 181
  Herbed Lima Bean Bake, 180
  Hot Five-Bean Salad, 145
  Marinated Three-Bean Salad, 144
  Quick Beans-and-Franks Soup, 166
  Quick Three-Bean Salad, 145
  Tongue and Lima Skillet, 108
Beef
  Beef Bourguignonne, 163
  Chef's Salad, 152
  Cider Stew, 164
  Creamed Dried Beef, 96
  Greek Salad, 151
  New England Boiled Dinner, 93
Beef, Ground
  Cocktail Meatballs, 9
  Hamburger Pie, 97
  Meatball Stew with Spinach Dumplings, 164
  Porcupine Meatballs, 98
  Quick Beef Goulash Stew, 164
  Skilletburgers, 96
Beef, Roasts
  Roast with Barbecue Gravy, 92
  Savory Stuffed Rib Roast, 92
  Teriyaki Roast Beef, 91
Beef, Steak
  Beef Teriyaki, 14
  Chicken-Fried Round Steak, 94
  Deviled Beef Rolls, 95
  London Broil, 94
  Onion-Stuffed Steak, 15
  Quick Garlic Cubed Steaks, 14
Beer Rabbit, 79
Beverages, 23-26
  Aricot Swizzle, 24
  Café Almond, 26
  Café Columbian, 26
  Café Israel, 26
  Dessert Coffee, 26
  Fruit Cooler, 25
  Fruit-Flavored Float, 25
  Hot Mulled Cider, 26
  Nonalcoholic Punch, 25

185

186 Index

Party Punch Base, 24
Strawberry Spritzer, 23
White Wine Punch, 24
Blonde Brownies, 56
Blue Cheese-Onion Dip, 12
Bordelaise Sauce, 159
Boston Brown Bread, 36
Bread Fix-Ups, Grilled, 21
Bread Pudding, 63
Breads, Quick, 31-38
  Apple Fritter Rings, 38
  Apple-Raisin Muffins, 33
  Banana-Nut Muffins, 33
  Basic Muffins, 32
  Boston Brown Bread, 36
  Cheese-Nut Bread, 35
  Cherry-Pecan Bread, 38
  Cranberry Muffins, 33
  Popovers, 33
  Spicy Buttermilk Coffee Cake, 36
  Streusel Coffee Cake, 37
  Three-C Bread, 34
  Zucchini Nut Loaf, 35
Breads, Yeast, 27-31
  Anadama Bread, 31
  Batter Rolls, 28
  Cheese Bread, 29
  Kuchen, 30
  Peasant Bread, 28
Broccoli
  Broccoli Oriental, 175
  Chicken Divan, 125
Brownies
  Blonde Brownies, 56
  Chocolate-Cream Cheese Brownies, 55
Busy-Day Cake, 40
Butterscotch Marble Cake, 42
C
Cabbage, Pennsylvania Red, 176
Café Almond, 26
Café Columbian, 26
Café Israel, 26
Cakes, 39-46
  Angel Cake, 44
  Applesauce Spice Cake, 41
  Busy-Day Cake, 40
  Butterscotch Marble Cake, 42
  Carrot Cake, 40
  Feathery Fudge Cake, 42
  German Chocolate Cake, 44
  Gingerbread, 43
  Golden Chiffon Cake, 46
  Hot Milk Sponge Cake, 45
Candied Squash Rings, 182
Candies, 49-52
  Chocolate Nut Balls, 50
  Choco-Scotch Crunchies, 50
  Cream Cheese Mints, 51
  Easy Fudge, 49
  Easy Walnut Penuche, 52

  Peppermint Bonbons, 52
Carrots
  Carrot Cake, 40
  Carrot-Rice Bake, 178
  Glazed Carrots, 174
Casseroles
  Classic Cheese Strata, 80
  Cottage Pasta Bake, 136
  Egg-Sausage Casserole, 73
  Eggs Florentine, 74
  Hamburger Pie, 97
  Mushroom-Cereal Bake, 138
  Mushroom-Rice Bake, 138
  Potato-Ham Scallop, 104
  Potluck Vegetable Casserole, 175
Casseroles, Fish
  Baked Fish with Mushrooms, 83
  Fish Florentine, 81
  Quick Fish-Potato Supper, 84
Casseroles, Poultry
  Chicken Divan, 125
  Crowd-Size Chicken Bake, 126
  Popover Chicken Tarragon, 129
  Wild-Rice-Chicken Casserole, 130
Cereal, 139-140
  Grits, 140
  Mushroom-Cereal Bake, 138
  Southern Cheese Grits, 140
  Spiced Porridge, 140
Cheese
  Beer Rabbit, 79
  Cheese Ball, 8
  Cheese Bread, 29
  Cheese French Omelet, 75
  Cheese-Nut Bread, 35
  Cheese Sauce, 156
  Cheese Soup, 170
  Cheese-Wine Log, 8
  Classic Cheese Fondue, 79
  Classic Cheese Strata, 80
  Cottage Pasta Bake, 136
  Easy Cheese Eggs à la King, 74
  Quick Cheesy Tuna Soup, 168
  Southern Cheese Grits, 140
  Welsh Rabbit, 78
Cheesecake, Sour Cream, 66
Cheesy Butter Spread, 22
Cheesy Chicken à la King, 122
Chef's Salad, 152
Cherries
  Cherry-Lemon Ring, 149
  Cherry-Pecan Bread, 38
  Fresh Cherry Pie, 112
Chicken
  Apricot Chicken, 124
  Cheesy Chicken à la King, 123
  Chef's Salad, 152
  Chicken à la King, 122
  Chicken-Asparagus Stacks, 128
  Chicken Divan, 125

Index

Chicken Fricassee, 124
Chicken Italiano, 120
Chicken Livers Stroganoff, 130
Chicken Paprikash, 119
Chicken Saltimbocca, 123
Chicken with Currant Glaze, 127
Cornmeal Batter Fried Chicken, 121
Crispy Baked Barbecue Chicken, 122
Crowd-Size Chicken Bake, 126
Curry and Parsley Chicken, 121
Glazed Chicken and Rice, 128
Oven-Crisped Orange Chicken, 126
Oven-Fried Chicken, 120
Parmesan Chicken, 120
Pineapple-Glazed Chicken, 16
Popover Chicken Tarragon, 129
Potato-Chip Chicken, 120
Roast Tarragon Chicken, 129
Wild-Rice-Chicken Casserole, 130
Chicken-Fried Round Steak, 94
Chinese Fried Rice, 139
Chocolate
Café Columbian, 26
Café Israel, 26
Chocolate Chiffon Pie, 118
Chocolate-Cream Cheese Brownies, 55
Chocolate Icing, 47
Chocolate Nut Balls, 50
Chocolate-Peanut Cookies, 57
Chocolate Pots de Crème, 66
Choco-Scotch Crunchies, 50
Easy Fudge, 49
Feathery Fudge Cake, 42
German Chocolate Cake, 44
Chowders (see Soups)
Cider Stew, 164
Cider Waldorf Mold, 148
Cinnamon Apple Rings, 162
Cocktail Meatballs, 9
Coconut
Broiled Coconut Topping, 48
Coconut Macaroons, 59
Coconut-Pecan Frosting, 48
Pineapple-Coconut Drops, 57
Coffee (see Beverages)
Coffee Cakes
Kuchen, 30
Spicy Buttermilk Coffee Cake, 36
Streusel Coffee Cake, 37
Coleslaw, Creamy, 147
Coleslaw, Vinaigrette, 147
Company Creamed Tuna, 86
Confetti Rice, 137
Confetti Sauce, 156
Cookies, Bar, 53, 54-56
Apricot-Filled Oatmeal Bars, 54
Blonde Brownies, 56
Chocolate-Cream Cheese Brownies, 55
Prune-Filled Oatmeal Bars, 54
Seven-Layer Bars, 56

Cookies, Drop, 53, 57-59
Basic Drop Cookies, 57
Chocolate-Peanut Cookies, 57
Coconut Macaroons, 59
Lemon Tea Cookies, 58
Lemon-Yogurt Cookies, 57
Pineapple-Coconut Drops, 57
Spicy Oatmeal-Raisin Cookies, 58
Cookies, Rolled and Refrigerated, 53-54, 61-62
Crisp Pecan Dainties, 61
Rolled Ginger Cookies, 62
Santa's Whiskers, 61
Cookies, Shaped, 53, 59-60
Almond Cookies, 59
Ginger Crinkles, 60
Sandies, 60
Corn
Corn Custard Pudding, 181
Corn-Stuffed Pork Chops, 17
Creamy Curried Corn, 180
Fresh Corn Chowder, 168
Cornmeal Batter-Fried Chicken, 121
Cottage Pasta Bake, 136
Crab
Boiled Crabs, 89
Crab Newburg, 90
Creole Gumbo, 165
Cranberries
Cranberry Muffins, 33
Cranberry-Orange Relish, 161
Tangy Cranberry Sauce, 9, 160
Cream Cheese Frosting, 47
Cream Cheese Mints, 51
Creamed Bratwurst, 106
Creamed Dried Beef, 96
Creamed Spinach with Nutmeg, 177
Creamed Vegetables, 173
Cream of Chicken Soup, 170
Creole Gumbo, 165
Crêpes
Basic Dessert Crêpes, 69
Crêpes Suzette, 68
Crisp Pecan Dainties, 61
Crispy Baked Barbecued Chicken, 122
Crowd-Size Chicken Bake, 126
Crunch Party Mix, 11
Cucumbers
Fresh Cucumber Relish, 162
Shrimp-Cucumber Appetizer Spread, 5
Sour Cream Cucumbers, 143
Curried Pork, 102
Curry and Parsley Chicken, 121
Custards (see Desserts)

D

Deep-Dish Peach Pie, 113
Denver Scramble, 72
Desserts, 63-70 (see also Cakes, Cookies, Pies)
Baked Alaska, 70

188 Index

Baked Apples, 68
Basic Dessert Crêpes, 69
Bread Pudding, 63
Chocolate Pots de Crème, 66
Crêpes Suzette, 68
Dessert Coffee, 26
Fresh Fruit Crisp, 65
Meringue Shells, 69
Praline Cheese Cups, 64
Saucepan Rice Pudding, 65
Sour Cream Cheesecake, 66
Stirred Custard, 64
Deviled Beef Rolls, 95
Deviled Eggs, 76
Dill
  Creamy Dill Dip, 11
  Dilled Lamb Ragout, 172
  Dilly Panned Summer Squash, 184
Dips
  Blue Cheese-Onion Dip, 12
  Creamy Dill Dip, 11
  Creamy Onion Dip, 12
  Fluffy Fruit Dip, 12

E
Eggplant, Spicy Stuffed, 183
Eggs
  Baked Eggs, 77
  Classic Quiche Lorraine, 76
  Denver Scramble, 72
  Deviled Eggs, 76
  Easy Cheese Eggs à la King, 74
  Egg Salad Triangles, 7
  Egg-Sausage Casserole, 73
  Eggs Benedict, 71
  Eggs Florentine, 74
  Farmer's Breakfast, 72
  French Omelet, 75
  Italian-Style Deviled Eggs, 76
  Mushroom French Omelet, 75
  Omelet Sandwich Puff, 78
  Vegetable French Omelet, 76

F
Farmer's Breakfast, 72
Feathery Fudge Cake, 42
Fish, 81-88
  Baked Tuna Patties, 86
  Company Creamed Tuna, 86
  Oven-Fried Fish, 84
  Salmon Loaf, 87
  Skillet Dilled Salmon Patties, 88
  Stacked Sole, 82
  Thawing, 82
Fish, Fillets and Steaks
  Baked Fillets and Steaks, 85
  Baked Fish à l'Orange, 85
  Baked Fish with Mushrooms, 83
Fish, Portions or Sticks
  Fish Florentine, 81
  Quick Fish-Potato Supper, 84
Foil-Barbecued Shrimp, 19

Fondue, Classic Cheese, 79
Frankfurters
  Polish Sausage-Krauters, 19
  Quick Beans-and-Franks Soup, 166
French Dressing, 154
French Omelet, 75
French Onion Soup, 171
Frostings, 46-48
  Broiled Coconut topping, 48
  Chocolate Icing, 47
  Coconut-Pecan Frosting, 48
  Cream Cheese Frosting, 47
  Fluffy White Frosting, 46
  Powdered Sugar Icing, 38
Fruit (see also individual fruits)
  Fluffy Fruit Dip, 12
  Fresh Fruit Crisp, 65
  Fruit Cooler, 25
  Fruit-Flavored Float, 25
  Fruit Strata Salad, 150
Fudge Cake, Feathery, 42
Fudge, Easy, 49

G
Garlic Cubed Steaks, Quick, 14
Garlic Spread, 22
Gazpacho Salad, 146
German Chocolate Cake, 44
German Sausage Chowder, 167
Gingerbread, 43
Ginger Cookies, Rolled, 62
Ginger Crinkles, 60
Glazed Carrots, 174
Glazed Chicken and Rice, 128
Glazed Ham Slice, 16
Golden Chiffon Cake, 46
Gravy, Pan, for Roast Poultry, 132
Greek Salad, 151
Green Beans Especial, 181
Green Goddess Dressing, 154
Green Goddess Salad, 142
Grits, 140
Grits, Southern Cheese, 140

H
Ham
  Apricot-Ham Patties, 104
  Baked Ham-Stuffed Mushrooms, 6
  Chef's Salad, 152
  Glazed Ham Slice, 16
  Ham Caribbean, 103
  Ham Hodgepodge, 169
  Party Ham Sandwiches, 7
  Potato-Ham Scallop, 104
  Swiss Cheese-Ham Spread, 8
Hamburger Pie, 97
Harvest Stuffing, 131
Herbed Lima Bean Bake, 180
Herbed Rice, 138
Herbed Spread, 22
Herb-Garlic Sauce, 156
Hollandaise Sauce, Classic, 157

Index

Hollandaise Sauce, Mock, 160
Horseradish Sauce, Fluffy, 159
Hot Mulled Cider, 26

I
Italian Dressing, 154
Italian-Seasoned Vegetable Kebabs, 21
Italian-Style Deviled Eggs, 76

K
Kuchen, 30

L
Lamb
  Dilled Lamb Ragout, 172
  Greek Salad, 151
  Lamb Chops Supreme, 106
  Lamb Loin Chops with Walnut Glaze, 108
  Saucy Lamb Shanks, 107
  Savory Lamburgers, 107
  Wine-Sauced Shoulder Chops, 20
Lemons
  Cherry-Lemon Ring, 149
  Lemon-Chess Pie, 117
  Lemon-Chive Sauce, 157
  Lemon Glaze, 58
  Lemon Pudding Cake, 67
  Lemon Tea Cookies, 58
  Lemon-Yogurt Cookies, 57
Lentil Soup, 167
Lima Bean Bake, Herbed, 180
Lima Skillet, Tongue and, 108
Lime Parfait Pie, 116
Livers, Chicken, Stroganoff, 130
Lobster
  Boiled Lobster Tails, 89
  Lobster Newburg, 90
London Broil, 94

M
Macaroons, Coconut, 59
Marinated Three-Bean Salad, 144
Meat (see Beef, Ham, Lamb, Pork, Veal)
Meatballs
  Cocktail Meatballs, 9
  Meatball Stew with Spinach Dumplings, 164
  Porcupine Meatballs, 98
Meatless Meal-in-a-Bowl, 152
Meringue Shells, 69
Microwave cooking
  Candied Squash Rings, 182
  Choco-Scotch Crunchies, 50
  Cooking Rice, 137
Milk
  Hot Milk Sponge Cake, 45
  Making Sour Milk, 37
Mint
  Cream Cheese Mints, 51
  Fresh Mint Sauce, 158
  Minted New Peas, 177
Mock Hollandaise Sauce, 160
Molded Shrimp Salad, 146

Muffins
  Apple-Raisin Muffins, 33
  Banana-Nut Muffins, 33
  Basic Muffins, 32
  Cranberry Muffins, 33
Mushrooms
  Baked Ham-Stuffed Mushrooms, 6
  Mushroom-Cereal Bake, 138
  Mushroom French Omelet, 75
  Mushroom-Rice Bake, 138
  Mushrooms Elegante, 182
  Mushroom Steak Sauce, 97

N
New England Boiled Dinner, 93
Nonalcoholic Punch, 25
Nut Bread, 34

O
Oatmeal
  Apricot-Filled Oatmeal Bars, 54
  Prune-Filled Oatmeal Bars, 54
  Spicy Oatmeal-Raisin Cookies, 58
Omelets
  Cheese French Omelet, 75
  French Omelet, 75
  Mushroom French Omelet, 75
  Omelet Sandwich Puff, 78
  Vegetable French Omelet, 76
Onions
  Creamy Onion Dip, 12
  French Onion Soup, 171
  Onion-Stuffed Steak, 15
Oranges
  Cranberry-Orange Relish, 161
  Orange-Glazed Ribs, 101
  Spinach-Orange Toss, 143
Oriental Vegetable Toss, 144
Oven-Browned Potatoes, 176
Oysters
  Oysters Rockefeller, 10
  Oyster Stew, 171

P
Pan Gravy for Roast Poultry, 132
Parmesan Chicken, 120
Parmesan Spread, 22
Parsley Rice, 137
Party Ham Sandwiches, 7
Party Punch Base, 24
Pasta
  Cottage Pasta Bake, 136
  Pasta with Carbonara Sauce, 135
  Pasta with Pesto, 134
  Spaghetti with Marinara Sauce, 134
Pastry
  Baked Pastry Shell, 110
  Pastry for Double-Crust Pie, 110
  Pastry for Lattice-Top Pie, 111
  Pastry for Single-Crust Pie, 110
Peaches
  Deep-Dish Peach Pie, 113
  Fresh Fruit Crisp, 65

Index

Pea Pods with Almonds, 178
Peas
  Minted New Peas, 177
  Sherry-Pea Soup Elegante, 172
  Split Pea Soup, 166
Peasant Bread, 28
Pennsylvania Red Cabbage, 176
Pesto, Pasta with, 134
Piecrusts (see Pastry)
Pies, Cream and Refrigerated
  Chocolate Chiffon Pie, 118
  Lemon-Chess Pie, 117
  Lime Parfait Pie, 116
Pies, Fruit
  Apple Crumble Pie, 111
  Apricot Pie, 112
  Deep-Dish Peach Pie, 113
  Fresh Cherry Pie, 112
  Fresh Pineapple Pie, 114
  Raisin Crisscross Pie, 114
  Rhubarb Pie, 116
  Strawberry Glacé Pie, 115
  Strawberry-Rhubarb Pie, 116
Pineapple
  Fresh Pineapple Pie, 114
  Pineapple-Coconut Drops, 57
  Pineapple-Glazed Chicken, 16
Polish Sausage-Krauters, 19
Popover Chicken Tarragon, 129
Popovers, 33
Porcupine Meatballs, 98
Pork
  Apple-Peanut-Buttered Pork Steaks, 18
  Basic Broiled Pork Chops and Steaks, 101
  Braised Pork Steaks, 100
  Curried Pork, 102
  Pork Burgers, 100
  Sweet-Sour Pork, 102
Potatoes
  Oven-Browned Potatoes, 176
  Potato-Chip Chicken, 120
  Potato-Ham Scallop, 104
  Potato Patties, 176
  Quick Fish-Potato Supper, 84
Potluck Vegetable Casserole, 175
Pot Roast, Sherried Veal, 98
Powdered Sugar Icing, 38
Praline Cheese Cups, 64
Prune-Filled Oatmeal Bars, 54
Puddings
  Bread Pudding, 63
  Corn Custard Pudding, 181
  Lemon Pudding Cake, 67
  Saucepan Rice Pudding, 65
Punches (see Beverages)

Q
Quiche Lorraine, Classic, 76
Quick Recipes
  Beans-and-Franks Soup, 166
  Beef Goulash Stew, 164
  Cheesy Tuna Soup, 168
  Fish-Potato Supper, 84
  Garlic Cubed Steaks, 14
  Three-Bean Salad, 145

R
Raisins
  Apple-Raisin Muffins, 33
  Raisin Crisscross Pie, 114
  Spicy Oatmeal-Raisin Cookies, 58
Relishes
  Cinnamon Apple Rings, 162
  Cranberry-Orange Relish, 161
  Fresh Cucumber Relish, 162
Rhubarb
  Rhubarb Pie, 116
  Strawberry-Rhubarb Pie, 116
Ribs
  Broiled Short Ribs, 95
  Orange-Glazed Ribs, 101
Rice
  Chinese Fried Rice, 139
  Confetti Rice, 137
  Cooking Rice, 137
  Herbed Rice, 138
  Mushroom-Rice Bake, 138
  Parsley Rice, 137
  Saucepan Rice Pudding, 65
Roast Tarragon Chicken, 129
Roast with Barbecue Gravy, 92
Russian Dressing, 154

S
Salad Dressings, 153-154
  Avocado Dressing, 153
  French Dressing, 154
  Green Goddess Dressing, 154
  Italian Dressing, 154
  Russian Dressing, 154
Salads, Fruit, 148-150
  Apricot Soufflé Salad, 148
  Cherry-Lemon Ring, 149
  Cider Waldorf Mold, 148
  Five-Cup Salad, 149
  Fruit Strata Salad, 150
Salads, Main-Dish, 150-153
  Chef's Salad, 152
  Greek Salad, 151
  Meatless Meal-in-a-Bowl, 152
  Scallop Toss, 153
  Shrimp-Avocado Salad, 150
Salads, Vegetable, 142-147
  Coleslaw Vinaigrette, 147
  Creamy Coleslaw, 147
  Gazpacho Salad, 146
  Green Goddess Salad, 142
  Hot Five-Bean Salad, 145
  Marinated Three-Bean Salad, 144
  Molded Shrimp Salad, 146
  Oriental Vegetable Toss, 144
  Quick Three-Bean Salad, 145
  Sour Cream Cucumbers, 143

Index

Spinach-Orange Toss, 143
Zucchini Salad Bowl, 142
Salmon
 Grilled Salmon Steaks, 18
 Salmon Loaf, 87
 Skillet Dilled Salmon Patties, 88
Sandwiches
 Omelet Sandwich Puff, 78
 Party Ham Sandwiches, 7
 Polish Sausage-Krauters, 19
 Pork Burgers, 100
 Savory Lamburgers, 107
 Skilletburgers, 96
Santa's Whiskers, 61
Saucepan Rice Pudding, 65
Sauces, 155-161
 Almond Sauce, 156
 Bordelaise Sauce, 159
 Cheese Sauce, 156
 Classic Hollandaise Sauce, 157
 Confetti Sauce, 156
 Easy Barbecue Sauce, 160
 Fluffy Horseradish Sauce, 159
 Fresh Mint Sauce, 158
 Herb-Garlic Sauce, 156
 Lemon-Chive Sauce, 157
 Mock Hollandaise Sauce, 160
 Mushroom Steak Sauce, 97
 Sauce Provençale, 158
 Sherry Sauce, 157
 Shrimp Sauce, 83
 Tangy Cranberry Sauce, 9, 160
 Tartar Sauce, 161
 White Sauce, 156
Saucy Lamb Shanks, 107
Sausage
 Creamed Bratwurst, 106
 Easy Pork Cassoulet, 166
 Egg-Sausage Casserole, 73
 German Sausage Chowder, 167
 Polish Sausage-Krauters, 19
 Sausage- and Apple-Stuffed Squash, 105
Savory Lamburgers, 107
Savory Stuffed Rib Roast, 92
Scalloped Vegetables, 173
Scallops
 Boiled Scallops, 89
 Scallop Toss, 153
Sesame Asparagus, 179
Seven-Layer Bars, 56
Shellfish (see also Crab, Lobster, Oysters, Scallops, Shrimp)
 Boiled Shellfish, 88
Sherried Veal Pot Roast, 98
Sherry-Pea Soup Elegante, 172
Sherry Sauce, 157
Short Ribs, Broiled, 95
Shrimp
 Boiled Shrimp, 88

Broiled Shrimp, 89
Creole Gumbo, 165
Foil-Barbecued Shrimp, 19
Molded Shrimp Salad, 146
Shrimp-Avocado Salad, 150
Shrimp-Cucumber Appetizer Spread, 5
Shrimp Newburg, 90
Shrimp-Rice Soup, 169
Shrimp Sauce, 83
Skilletburgers, 96
Skillet Dilled Salmon Patties, 88
Soups, Main-Dish
 Cream of Chicken Soup, 170
 Creole Gumbo, 165
 German Sausage Chowder, 167
 Ham Hodgepodge, 169
 Quick Beans-and-Franks Soup, 166
 Shrimp-Rice Soup, 169
Soups, Meal-Mate
 Cheese Soup, 170
 French Onion Soup, 171
 Fresh Corn Chowder, 168
 Lentil Soup, 167
 Quick Cheesy Tuna Soup, 168
 Sherry-Pea Soup Elegante, 172
 Split Pea Soup, 166
Sour Cream Cheesecake, 66
Sour Cream Cucumbers, 143
Spaghetti with Marinara Sauce, 134
Spiced Porridge, 140
Spicy Buttermilk Coffee Cake, 36
Spicy Oatmeal-Raisin Cookies, 58
Spicy Stuffed Eggplant, 183
Spinach
 Creamed Spinach with Nutmeg, 177
 Meatball Stew with Spinach Dumplings, 164
 Spinach-Orange Toss, 143
Split Pea Soup, 166
Squash
 Candied Squash Rings, 182
 Dilly Panned Summer Squash, 184
 Grilled Acorn Squash, 20
 Sausage- and Apple-Stuffed Squash, 105
Stacked Sole, 82
Stews
 Beef Bourguignonne, 163
 Cider Stew, 164
 Dilled Lamb Ragout, 172
 Easy Pork Cassoulet, 166
 Meatball Stew with Spinach Dumplings, 164
 Oyster Stew, 171
 Quick Beef Goulash Stew, 164
Stirred Custard, 64
Strata, Classic Cheese, 80
Strawberries
 Strawberry Glacé Pie, 115
 Strawberry Rhubarb Pie, 116

Strawberry Spritzer, 23
Streusel Coffee Cake, 37
Stuffing, Harvest, 131
Sweet-Sour Pork, 102
Swiss Cheese-Ham Spread, 8

T
Tangy Cranberry Sauce, 9, 160
Tartar Sauce, 161
Teriyaki Roast Beef, 91
Three-Bean Salad, Marinated, 144
Three-Bean Salad, Quick, 145
Three-C Bread, 34
Tomatoes
    Baked Tomatoes, 184
    Broiled Tomatoes, 184
Tongue and Lima Skillet, 108
Tuna
    Baked Tuna Patties, 86
    Company Creamed Tuna, 86
    Quick Cheesy Tuna Soup, 168
Turkey, Cooked
    Chef's Salad, 152
    Chicken-Asparagus Stacks, 128
    Crowd-Size Chicken Bake, 126

V
Veal
    Sherried Veal Pot Roast, 98
    Veal Cordon Bleu, 99
Vegetables (see also individual vegetables)
    Au Gratin Vegetables, 173
    Creamed Vegetables, 173
    Italian-Seasoned Vegetable Kebabs, 21
    Potluck Vegetable Casserole, 175
    Scalloped Vegetables, 173
    Vegetable French Omelet, 76

W
Walnut Penuche, Easy, 52
Welsh Rabbit, 78
White Sauce, 156
White Wine Punch, 24
Wild-Rice-Chicken Casserole, 130
Wine-Sauced Shoulder Chops, 20

Y-Z
Yogurt Cookies, Lemon-, 57
Zucchini
    Italian-Seasoned Vegetable Kebabs, 21
    Zucchini Nut Loaf, 35
    Zucchini Salad Bowl, 142